J. KENNETH MORRIS

PREMARITAL COUNSELING

A *manual for ministers*

PRENTICE-HALL, INC.   *Englewood Cliffs, N. J.*
MCMLX

20764

*D*edicated to my wife, whose love and understanding have made our marriage such a happy and successful one that this book could be written.

Preface

If an architect suggested building a home on a quicksand base, or a doctor advised incantations as a cancer cure, the public would write them off as quacks and seek intelligent advice. Yet, many couples approach marriage with little better instruction, believing that a foundation of physical attraction and the recitation of vows fill all requirements for a happy marriage.

The results of this lack of preparation for marriage lie behind the development of this manual, which has been in process many years. It has grown out of three convictions: (1) that the increase in unhappy marriages and the divorce rate pose a demand on the Church to see that all couples married in the Church are given premarital counseling; (2) evidence by ministers and married couples that this is not being done sufficiently; (3) that the average minister lacks an adequate concept of premarital counseling and its techniques.

This manual provides ministers with suggestions for premarital counseling which will help couples build happy and successful marriages. For out of such marriages will come men and women of sufficient emotional stability to enable them to build cells of the Kingdom of God in their homes through wholesome interpersonal relationships. Sick marriages release to the Church and society sick individuals with warped personalities, unable to adjust adequately in their relationships with others. These marriages turn out many neurotics who, in turn, marry neurotics and thus perpetuate the process. The procedures suggested for premarital counseling are the result of the author's experience of more than a decade as a marriage counselor.

The churches, gravely concerned about marriage and the family, are becoming more and more aware of the need for premarital counseling and the subjects which it should cover. The attitudes of the churches are reflected in the laws, statements, and regulations of the Protestant Episcopal Church, the Methodist Church, the Presbyterian Church in the United States, the United Lutheran Church of America, and in the Lambeth Conference of the Bishops of the Anglican Communion. Their documents are quoted in the Appendices.

Technical psychological terms and discussion of highly specialized devices used by professional counselors have been omitted from the manual. In most cases, these are not suited to the needs of the minister-counselor. Only a Background Schedule and the Sex Knowledge Inventory, Form X are recommended for him. As greater competence is gained through counseling experience, the minister may wish to use tests such as personality inventories and prediction scales.

All biblical quotations used are from the Revised Standard Version of the Bible, copyrighted 1946 and 1952 by the Division of Christian Education of the National Council of Churches and used by permission.

I am deeply indebted to those who have given me encouragement and help in developing the material and in preparing the manuscript. I wish particularly to express my appreciation for the valuable suggestions and criticisms of Elmore A. Martin, Ph.D., Chief Psychologist, South Carolina State Hospital, and Carl A. Bramlette, Jr., Ph.D., Psychology Consultant, South Carolina Mental Health Commission; also to Erland N. P. Nelson, Ph.D., Professor of Psychology, University of South Carolina; and Mrs. Ethel M. Nash, M.A., Member, American Association of Marriage Counselors, and Family Life Specialist at the Bowman-Gray School of Medicine, Winston-Salem, North Carolina. I am also indebted to Mrs. Claude H. Neuffer, M.A., for reading the manuscript for composition and style, and to Mrs. Wayland H. Davis for the typing. For errors of omission and commission which may be discovered I am solely responsible.

J. KENNETH MORRIS

Contents

I

THE NEED

xi

II

THE APPROACH

III

METHODS

V

THE OVERVIEW

APPENDICES

*in the United States enacted by the General Assembly 1959 · The
Book of Church Order 1945 · Statement added to paragraph 376,
General Assembly 1959*

I

THE NEED

1

The Church's dependence upon healthy marriage relationships

The Church, like the State, is dependent upon the family as an integral part of its structure. But the family, being the cradle of the individual, is capable of providing the Church with strong, weak, or mediocre members; for it is in the family that men and women are first conditioned physiologically, psychologically, and sociologically to meet the stress and strain of life.

So far as the Church is concerned, there is no substitute for healthy marriages. Many defections from the Church's standards of behavior come out of "sick" marriages. Marriages can and do become sick just as do individuals. A strong, stable, wholesome marriage tends to produce a person who is capable of withstanding the pull of conflicting interests that enter into the varied relationships existing in any social order. Thus, a stable marriage develops stress tolerance through the cooperative efforts of the family group.

3

Married persons appear to be considerably less susceptible to the development of psychotic disorders than the widowed, single, and divorced. . . . Stress tolerance is undoubtedly strengthened by the teamwork, group identification, and mutual emotional support received in a healthy marriage. Family life brings interesting and stable social relations, and thus can alleviate feelings of isolation and individual helplessness; and child-rearing brings self-obliterating responsibilities and duties and the feeling of being needed.[1]

Christian marriage defined

When one speaks of a Christian marriage, just what does one have in mind? A church wedding blessed by a minister? Does the minister possess some magic that automatically makes a marriage Christian? We may define a Christian marriage as one involving a Christian man and woman, each dedicated to his understanding of God's purpose for him and to helping his spouse and their children to achieve the measure of the fullness of the stature of Christ. In a marriage that is truly Christian, both the husband and wife will respect the developing personality of the other, aid its enhancement, strengthen it wherever weak, encourage it in its goodness—anticipating old age when both may present themselves to each other, without spot or blemish, even as Christ presents the Church, His spouse, to Himself.

To those outside the Church, we may be speaking in mystic language, but to those within the Church, whose frame of reference is Christ, the meaning should be clear. It should also be clear to every Christian minister that he has a grave responsibility in preparing young people to achieve this ideal of marriage. Such a marriage does not just happen, there has to be the ideal and the willingness to work to make it a reality. With the rising divorce rate, we may conclude that even some Christian marriages —or should we say "church weddings"—result in unhappy homes, with more and more people becoming alienated from the Church.

[1] James C. Coleman, *Abnormal Psychology and Modern Life* (Chicago: Scott, Foresman and Company © 1950), p. 225.

The Christian home begins in the Church

Those couples who come to the minister to be married should know that the Christian home begins in the Church and that the minister has the duty and the privilege of helping them start their marriage on the road to success. The minister has a great responsibility to work for the establishment of homes which will develop well-adjusted individuals who are capable of becoming happy Christians, able to walk in God's way throughout their lives, enjoying a wholesome relationship with their neighbors. Sick marriages produce sick people with sick minds and sick bodies.

Therefore, the minister must recognize the place of premarital counseling in his pastoral work. He must understand the need for it, the problems he must deal with, and the techniques[2] he may use.

Good and bad patterns of behavior learned in the family

Many families fail to produce the kind of Christian the Church teaches her children to become. Unless the average child is conditioned in the home to make good physiological, psychological, and sociological adjustments, he may be unable to fulfill his Christian obligations when he becomes an adult. Good and bad patterns of behavior are learned by children in the family and are carried over into adulthood and thence into their own marriages. Neurotic marriages tend to produce neurotic individuals. They in turn, often marry neurotics, and the pattern is duplicated in another generation. The Church is concerned with both "healthy" and "sick" marriages, because the members of those families may also be members of the Church. Parents who have never experienced Christian living in their childhood homes can hardly impart it to their children.

[2] It is not the purpose of this manual to cover the techniques of counseling in general. There are many books which deal with the subject adequately. See the bibliography.

Personality structure, tough but delicately adjusted

Generally speaking, the personality structure of an individual is tough enough to withstand many shocks and overcome serious traumatic experiences; otherwise, we should have more people in our mental institutions than on the outside. But the personality structure is also like the mechanism of a fine precision instrument, which, if not handled in accordance with its function and the rules of operation, can be thrown out of gear by some clumsy or uninstructed operator. One's digestive system is remarkable in its ability to digest a great variety of "experiences" with all kinds of food. If it is overloaded, or if we unthinkingly cram it with unprepared food or extraneous matter, the reaction in the system can be quite violent and may result in permanent damage. The personality structure is analogous to the digestive system in the sense that it, too, can be overloaded with abuse, denied understanding, or be so surrounded by an emotionally charged environment that the reaction may be violent; a permanently warped condition may result.

We know that just as children in school are taught the functions of the digestive system and the principles of good physical hygiene, they must also be taught the basic principles of good mental health. They must have daily opportunity to practice them, correct their mistakes and thrill over their successes. They need to know that there is such a thing as a personality structure even though the theories about its nature differ. If they are to build wholesome, healthy relationships with other people, they must understand how interpersonal relationships are affected by both objective and subjective attitudes toward one's environment.

These interpersonal relationships within the family are most vital in creating an environment in which strong personality structures can be built. The minister has many opportunities to be the first to instruct a couple in the elementary dynamics of personality development and in the importance of creating a harmonious,

healthy and happy environment for the children who result from
the marriage.

Not all handicaps overcome by faith

Children may be handicapped in their psychological and sociological patterns of adjustment to life, just as they may be at a
disadvantage because of some physical impairment. We generally
accept the physically handicapped person as capable of making
only a partial adjustment, and we know that the mentally retarded
person may be able to make some adjustment also. We can accept
the limitations that may come to a child who has met with an accident and lost his leg. We do not pray God to grow another leg.
Some may say the accident was the will of God (though how
anyone could possibly think of God as willingly afflicting any of
his children is beyond my comprehension).

We blindly believe that a person who was mistreated or rejected
by his parents in childhood should, by his baptism, confirmation,
joining the Church, or profession of faith, suddenly become an
obedient, loving child of his heavenly Father and walk in His way
for the rest of his life. While daring to hope and pray that he
may, we immediately provide Confession and Absolution for the
sins he will commit. This is right, for no one lives perfectly.
Too often we fail to recognize the basic personality defects which
cause defections from the faith and Christian standards, and we
do nothing to help the individual understand himself and his problems. Being a loyal church member (as indicated by regular
attendance, participating in church activities, and contributing to
its support) does not mean one loves his neighbor as himself, is
honest in his business, or gets along happily in his marriage.

An acquaintance who was trying to make his way in the Church
but having a difficult time because of his over-protective and domineering mother, described her as a very devout, loyal church woman.
She went to church regularly on Sunday, taking the family with

her. She was a model of piety in her acts of worship. "But," he added, "when she got home all hell broke loose!" This man had been a member of the Church all his early life, but had long since stopped going. Now, however, he needed the strong, stabilizing influence of religion to reinforce his super-ego and help him to meet a serious moral problem by saying "No" to temptation and meaning it. He could not make terms with religion until he came to understand his feelings toward the Church which involved his attitude toward his mother. Since childhood he had been psychologically handicapped in accepting religion.

Just as faith in Christ cannot replace a child's lost leg, neither can faith in Christ bring about a fundamental change in a personality where there are psychological impairments equally as serious. We no longer expect God to do this for the mentally retarded child suffering from brain injury. Many physical handicaps of children can now be corrected, or even prevented, through the advances of medical science. We can also assist those who are psychologically handicapped. Psychology has a great deal to offer which will enable men and women to be better Christians, well adjusted and happy in their religious associations. However, the foundation for sound psychological and sociological health, like physical health, is laid in the home.

Persistence of childhood patterns of behavior

The particular patterns of behavior developed in childhood to deal with frustrations continue throughout life. Of course, we modify them. We no longer throw a tantrum by lying on the floor and kicking and screaming; instead, we may slam the door, throw down a book, or spend the evening sulking. Some do, of course, revert to more juvenile reactions and yell their words, curse, and hit.

"Scratch the adult and you will find the child" is a modern cliché in psychology. In times of sudden crisis we lose some of our inhibitions and revert to childhood patterns of behavior.

From infancy onward, the individual's reaction to a present stimulus (a crisis such as a death, disappointment, etc.) is a function in the main, of his reactions to past stimuli. Characteristics develop or change little by little over a period of time, with few exceptions. Even in the case of catastrophic changes in personality (such as conversion, mental illness, etc.) it is usually possible to show how the person's past training prepared him to respond in his characteristic way to a crisis situation.[3]

Although it is obvious that marriage is for emotionally mature adults, there are many who approach marriage unaware of the childish personality traits they are bringing with them: traits which they acquired from infancy in the home or in whatever environment in which they may have been reared—an orphanage, training school, boarding school, or foster home.

During courtship a couple may get along quite well—encouraged by the saying "the course of true love never runs smooth"—and fail to analyze the reasons for whatever disagreements they may have, or criticisms made of each other. These points of friction are important and quite revealing of the inner organization of the individual. After marriage, when the effort of courting and winning each other has ended, the real self begins to be revealed more and more with the result that friction will be more frequent and serious. Just because one is an adult does not mean one is emotionally mature.

Emotional give and take in marriage

Spouses must be of emotional value to each other. As adults they must be able to give emotionally of themselves through mutual dependence, acceptance of responsibility, mature sexual and love responses, and whatever else may be required to satisfy the needs of each personality as it seeks to adjust to the environment. If spouses are not of value to each other emotionally, or if one is and the other is not, a strong successful marriage cannot result. Of

[3] Ross Stagner, *Psychology of Personality* (New York: McGraw-Hill Book Company, Inc. © 1948), p. 14. Reprinted by permission.

course, one spouse may use the other, give nothing of emotional value in return and consider the marriage a fair one. This is using the other person for selfish ends. It is contrary to the Christian ideal of the intrinsic worth of the individual for what he is and not for the use someone may make of him. Some women say of their husbands, "All that he seems to want of me is sex." Or, husbands say that their wives use them only for material security. It is often said that the immature person uses people and loves things; the mature person loves people and uses things.

In premarital counseling the skilled counselor can do much to help a couple analyze their points of friction and come to a better understanding of themselves.

A case of jealousy based on immaturity

A typical case may be cited. In her first premarital interview, the girl stated her concern with her fiance's jealousy. He seemed to resent any boy's speaking to her, or her being friendly with any boys. She had been a popular girl with many beaux and, being of an outgoing personality, she wanted to retain their friendship. But, whenever she spoke to any of them or met them even casually on the street, her fiance would express his feelings quite strongly and then sulk, sometimes accusing her of flirting or of caring more for their companionship than for his. They had had some very upsetting quarrels about this and she had even thought of breaking off the engagement.

When the young man came for his first interview and was asked, "Have you and Mary had any quarrels during your engagement period?" he replied with vehemence, "Yes, she is too friendly with other men. I have accused her of flirting with them. She belongs to me, and I don't want her having anything to do with other men."

As we discussed this problem, it soon developed that he was very dependent on his mother, with some resentment toward his father, whom he felt was a threat to his closeness with his mother. Also, he had had a previous engagement, which had been broken by the girl who fell in love with and married someone else. This experience, which left him very depressed and unhappy, threw him back upon his mother's love and sympathy. He had not received aid from his father in this crisis to help him adjust to it; instead, his father seemed to become even more of a threat to his dependence on his mother.

Now he had fallen in love again. The girl was much more mature and independent than he was, quite like his mother. Every boy who spoke to her became a threat to his closeness with her. She might fall in love and leave him as the first girl had done; and these men might try to come between him and his mother (seen in the girl). When he began to see the whole picture objectively and with some understanding of the girl's personality, he realized that he could trust her love for him. Learning to discriminate between the girl and his mother, and himself as lover and son, he soon began to lose his jealousy and, to the girl's surprise, began to be friendly with the very men of whom he had been jealous. Without premarital counseling this couple may have broken up, or their marriage may have been a continual wrangling over his wife's friends.

The early environment

Sociological health is dependent, also, upon the kind of social environment created in the home, because it is there that fundamental social learning begins. In the home, children learn to cooperate in the interest of a common goal and to make sacrifices to promote the welfare of the family. They also learn that people have different opinions on a variety of subjects and that healthy social intercourse is dependent upon one's being ready to listen to and respect opinions divergent from one's own. The home is society in miniature. It can be easily demonstrated to the child that anti-social behavior—such as stealing cookies, lying, or failing to do his chores—disrupts the smooth social life which should prevail, just as in adult society violators of the law cause deep concern and expense to the state. Learning to be a part of one's social environment, without accepting its ugly features, and finding creative ways of improving it can be taught to a child, not by rote, but by the daily experience shared within the home. The Christian ideal of marriage needs to be more clearly defined.

Summary

What we need to understand as ministers is that the Christian character we seek to develop in church members, as well as in society as a whole, must be rooted in the physiological, psychological and sociological just as much as in the religious conditions of the home. There is no such thing as a suspended Christian. He comes out of a foundation of some sort. The "pay dirt" is the environment of a healthy marriage. Sound mental health is an essential ingredient in the highest order of Christian character.

But this goal must be planned and striven for. It does not just happen for the majority of people. There are personality structures strong enough to withstand amazing environmental disturbances. These will take care of themselves as they always have done. In this scientific age the Church has no right to leave succeeding generations of her children to chance. Premarital counseling can help couples form marriages, out of which will issue mentally healthy children who will be capable of developing wholesome, creative relationships with others and thereby help build the Kingdom of God.

II

THE APPROACH

2

Premarital counseling

Premarital counseling defined

Premarital counseling is that form of counseling which centers around the interpersonal relationship of a man and a woman, helps them evaluate their relationship in view of their approaching marriage and acquaints them with ways by which they may build a happy and successful marriage, or, in the light of the evaluation of their relationship, results in their deciding against the marriage.

Premarital counseling encompasses at least the main areas in which couples have been found to have their greatest difficulty. According to Judson T. and Mary G. Landis, the areas of greatest difficulty in working out a satisfactory adjustment are sex relations, spending the family income, social activities, in-law relationships, religious activities, and mutual friends.[1] In premarital counseling,

---

[1] Judson T. Landis, "Length of Time Required to Achieve Adjustment in Marriage," *American Sociological Review*, 11:6 (December, 1946), p. 668. Reprinted in Judson T. and Mary G. Landis, *Building a Successful Marriage*, 3rd ed. (Englewood Cliffs, N.J.: Prentice-Hall, Inc., 1958), p. 356.

the possible difficulties which commonly arise in these areas are discussed realistically in relation to the peculiarities of each individual against his educational, social, and psychological background with the hypothesis that clear, objective thinking in these areas before marriage in the permissive atmosphere of the counseling relationship may aid toward a solution of any problems which may arise after marriage or may even prevent many problems from arising.

Premarital counseling distinguished from other counseling

Premarital counseling in the Church differs from other counseling in that (1) most of the couples the minister counsels will come at his insistence rather than on their own initiative, and (2) considerable instruction as well as counseling is involved in it.   Very likely the couples will not understand what premarital counseling is.

They may have in mind some vague notion that the minister will explain the details of the ceremony.   Therefore, they do not come of their own accord to consult him about personal problems. The girl may come in the first instance to tell her minister that she plans to marry and wants him to perform the ceremony. Sometimes the mother takes this preliminary step for the girl.

This is the time to explain—though we hope our young people will soon come to expect it—that the Church requires the minister to instruct the couples he marries in the nature of Holy Matrimony, or Christian marriage; and that in order to do this, he must see the couple together to discuss the marriage and the instruction he will give.

Importance of ventilating in premarital counseling

Premarital counseling gives opportunity for individuals to talk about themselves, their families, and sweethearts.   In this way their feelings may be ventilated.   Few people have ever had an opportunity to talk over their psychological problems with a person unemotionally related to them and their problems. They seem to welcome this opportunity and time and again express great relief over having gotten certain things off their chests. For the understanding pastor this often establishes a close personal relationship with the individual.

It is our observation that most young people want to understand their emotional responses to various situations, but do not know to whom to talk. They do not want lecturing, or moralizing, but rather crave understanding of their feelings and actions. The counselor should not sit in judgment, condemn, or use the counselee as an audience to listen to his own experiences. His approach is to create a permissive atmosphere in which the counselee will feel free to discuss any matters without fear that the minister will express shock or condemnation, will lecture, or will attempt to compare each of the counselee's experiences with one of the counselor's more colorful experiences.

In the pamphlet, *Counseling Service,* Dr. Aaron L. Rutledge says:

Neither counseling nor psychotherapy is advice-giving, but rather a relationship in which counselor and client share in the responsibility of understanding the self, learning to feel differently about that which is necessary to change, and finding ways of stimulating the processes of growth and development. Counseling is a "learning process" through which the individual is aided in finding ways to deal with his own problems and in beginning to realize more fully his potential as an effective person.[2]

Confidence essential

Of course, what the counselor is told must be kept in confidence. Case histories mentioned in this text have been so disguised (without changing the basic facts) as to make the detection of the persons impossible. Some case histories are mixed where that has made it possible to cover several points.

[2] Aaron L. Rutledge, *Counseling Service* (Detroit, Mich.: The Merrill-Palmer School).

Classification of couples

Those who come for premarital counseling fall into certain groups:

1. The emotionally mature who are in good health and who come from wholesome homes in which they have learned to make good psychological and sociological adjustments. Counseling with these individuals is usually a source of great pleasure for the minister. The wedding puts a seal upon a good relationship that should ripen through the years.

2. Mismatched couples who already, before marriage, have various maladjustments in their relations with each other. These are often immature and emotionally unstable individuals. Although the minister cannot escape his responsibility in counseling these couples, he must be prepared for doubts as to the success of their marriage. Sometimes they come to realize that they are not suited for each other and decide against marriage. But the chances are that they will marry each other despite their maladjustments. Therefore, the premarital counseling must help them to be realistic about their differences and conflicts, accepting in each what may not be changed. However, some of these couples make remarkable changes under skilled counseling.

3. The physically sick or handicapped who have chronic, latent or active diseases, or who have had hysterectomies or disfiguring operations. All such persons should have a thorough physical examination before the personal interviews begin. The minister-counselor has a real opportunity to assist such individuals and their spouses to accept their handicaps and to become a working team. Some of the noblest examples of Christian marriage have come out of such unions which call for love's self-sacrifice in unlimited devotion.

4. The neurotic or psychotic who are unsuited to marriage until they have had psychotherapy. Some of them, even then, will be unable to assume the responsibilities of married life and parent-

hood. The counselor should be able to recognize such persons and refer them for psychiatric help. In this category we also put the untreated alcoholics, drug addicts, and those who show continuing anti-social behavior or who have criminal records.

Content and number of interviews

The premarital counseling varies somewhat in content and number of interviews, depending on the couple. Some couples have already received very good instruction in their college courses; some have read carefully books on the family and Christian marriage. Others have been reared in homes where the full meaning of Christian marriage was set before them daily by precept and example. Then, of course, there are those who know practically nothing about marriage and its responsibilities and some who have a very crude idea of marriage, looking on it as a matter of convenience in providing the material comforts of a home, but devoid of real companionship; while others think of it largely in terms of sexual gratification.

We have found through experience that a minimum of eight interviews is required for each couple. These consist of the following:

1. The first interview with the couple together.

2. At least three personal interviews with each person depending upon the problems presented by him.

3. A final interview with the couple together.

These interviews last an hour to an hour and a half. In addition interviews may be required with prospective in-laws as suggested in this Manual. (*See* Chapter 8.)

Conflicts are real but not fatal

Before marriage each partner tends to oversell himself. Many latent differences between the lovers do not show up until after the honeymoon when they begin the routine of living together daily. They soon find that adjustments in many areas must be made and that to make a success of their marriage they must work out these adjustments with patience and understanding. It would be unreal if conflicts did not occur. The two people come from backgrounds that differ in many respects: family customs, traditions, ways in which parents resolved their conflicts, child training practices, and many other aspects of family life—to say nothing of cultural, economic and social differences. Premarital counseling helps them evaluate their cultural heritages so that when conflicts arise they will not prove fatal to the marriage.

Hypothesis and survey

Premarital counseling should result in a high percentage of happy marriages. This hypothesis has not been thoroughly investigated and cannot be until there are more couples who have had structured premarital counseling and who have been married at least 10 years. Since 55 per cent of divorces take place in the first 10 years of marriage, couples married a full 10 years who have received premarital counseling would provide a fair sample of an experimental group.

The author attempted such a study in 1957 based on an experimental group of 41 couples whom he had counseled before marriage, and a control group of 186 white couples who had been married in Episcopal churches of a large southern city.[3] The shortest term of marriage in each group was one year and the longest 10 years. Since premarital counseling is a relatively new field, a survey of those who have received such counseling must, in most cases, be limited to couples whose period of married life has been short. Although for years many ministers have held brief conferences with couples before marriage, a scientific approach to premarital counsel-

[3] J. Kenneth Morris, "A Study of Premarital Counseling in Relation to a Survey of Marital Adjustment" (Master's thesis, University of South Carolina, 1957).

ing is quite recent. At the time of the 1957 study, the author had been giving premarital counseling for only 11 years, necessitating his limiting the experimental group to couples with from one to 10 years of married life.

Subjects were asked to rate their marriage in regard to marital happiness on a five-point scale: very happy, happy, average, unhappy, very unhappy. Of the individuals reporting in the experimental group, 72.1 per cent rated their marriage as very happy, and 27.9 per cent as happy. None rated their marriage lower than happy. In the control group, 61.2 per cent rated their marriage as very happy; 32.8 per cent as happy; 4.5 per cent, average; 1.5 per cent, unhappy.

These results were compared with a study by Landis[4] of 818 spouses who had been married 20 years. Landis' couples, although not asked if they had received premarital counseling, most certainly would not have received it prior to 1928. Of these individuals, 48.2 per cent reported their marriages as very happy; 34.6 per cent happy; 16.4 per cent average; and eight-tenths per cent unhappy.

Would the subjects in the experimental group lower the rating in another 10 to 20 years? Terman found no indication of a drop in happiness after 20 years. In fact, he found a very low correlation between happiness scores and length of marriage.[5]

As the subject matter of premarital counseling is better defined and techniques developed, it is hoped that further surveys will be made and prediction schedules formulated which will be of great value to minister-counselors in their efforts to help their young couples form lasting and happy marriages. From our survey we conclude that premarital counseling is effective in helping couples make happy marriages.

Edmund Bergler writes:

[4] Judson T. Landis, "Length of Time Required to Achieve Adjustment in Marriage," *American Sociology Review*, 11:6 (December, 1946), p. 674.

[5] Lewis Terman, *Psychological Factors in Marital Happiness* (New York: McGraw-Hill Book Company, Inc. © 1938), p. 175. Used with publisher's permission.

Many marriages are condemned to failure from the start because of the impossible unconscious expectations with which people enter into them, and especially because of the neurotic behavior of the partners. The inner problem of divorce does not begin on the day when the married couple, full of rage, or hate, or with tears of regret, decide to dissolve the marriage, but much earlier. Thus the problem of how divorce in bad marriages is to be prevented is reduced to how good marriages can be promoted.[6]

Premarital counseling seeks to promote good marriages. Its aim is to aid couples in making successful marital adjustments without these adjustments becoming threats to the stability of the home. If the nature of the adjustments is understood so that couples realize the possible obstacles to these adjustments, adjustments will usually come early in the marriage and consequently will strengthen the marriage bonds and reduce the divorce rate. Premarital counseling is, therefore, preventive therapy against sick marriages and divorce.

The Church's responsibility recognized

The Church's responsibility for the instruction of couples in preparation for marriage has been recognized by several churches, some requiring it in church law.

The Protestant Episcopal Church. This church requires of the minister before he solemnize any marriage that "He shall have instructed the parties as to the nature of Holy Matrimony" and that "the intention of the parties to contract a marriage shall have been signified to the Minister at least three days before the service of solemnization." (*See* Appendix I.)

The Anglican Communion. The Committee Report on the Family in Contemporary Society made at the Lambeth Conference of 1958 for Bishops of the Anglican Communion (which includes the Protestant Episcopal Church in the United States of America) states:

[6] Edmund Bergler, *Unhappy Marriage and Divorce* (New York: International Universities Press, 1946), p. 11.

It will be generally agreed that the most valuable contribution the Church can make toward the stability of the marriage bond is to help young people to marry in the right way. This is very largely the responsibility of the parochial clergy. We would urge all our provinces to provide for premarital interviews between pastors and people concerned, where instruction can be given, along the lines of this report, in the nature of marriage and family life and their problems. Where specialized physical or other counsel is needed, such interviews can well discover the need, and provide means to meet it. They will be spiritual opportunities for young people who are about to make solemn promises to each other and to God, who will and do welcome such help. In explaining the meaning of the marriage service and its implications, pastors are provided with unique opportunities of relating the whole Christian faith to the lives of such people.[7]

The Methodist Church. The portion of its Discipline governing the Ministry states that "In planning to perform the rite of matrimony the minister is advised to have an unhurried premarital conference with the parties to be married. It is strongly urged that the minister advise and instruct to the best of his ability to the end that the parties to be married become soberly aware that successful marriage is dependent on those spiritual qualities which are best nurtured and kept alive by a constant sense of loyalty to God and to God's organized Church." [8]

A resolution adopted by the General Conference of the Methodist Church indicates the emphasis Church leaders place upon the importance of the Church doing all in its power to point out to its members the meaning of Christian marriage and to help them build successful marriages. (*See* Appendix II.) Marriage is an achievement, and as such it must be prepared for adequately and the emotional adjustments required for a happy marriage must be understood in advance. The Methodist Church in support of its

[7] *The Lambeth Conference 1958* (Greenwich, Conn.: Society for Promoting Christian Knowledge and Seabury Press, 1958), *p. 2.155.*

[8] *Doctrines and Discipline of the Methodist Church* (Nashville, Tenn.: The Methodist Publishing House, © 1957 by the Board of Publication of the Methodist Church, Incorporated), p. 130.

efforts to encourage pastors in the preparation of couples for marriage has put out an official publication, *The Pastor's Manual for Premarital Counseling*. It is planned specifically as a companion to *In Holy Matrimony*, the official marriage manual of the Methodist Church for engaged couples.

The Presbyterian Church in the United States. In the General Assembly of 1959 this church adopted the following recommendation:

It shall be the responsibility of the minister who is asked to officiate at a marriage to provide adequate time for careful premarital counseling with the parties involved. Attention shall be given to all important aspects of marriage, especially those where problems may arise, whether they be physical, emotional, economic, social, moral or religious. In some instances the minister may deem it wise to refer the couple to a physician or other qualified person for special counseling. The minister shall carefully instruct the couple in the Standards of our Church as set forth in Chapter XXVI of *The Confession of Faith* and in this chapter of *The Directory for Worship*. [See Appendix III.] This counseling procedure shall be followed not only for those contemplating marriage for the first time, but also for any who may be seeking remarriage. In every instance it shall be the minister's duty to assist the couple in laying firm foundations for the establishment of a Christian home.

Attention of the minister-counselor is directed to the Bible references noted in Chapter XXVI of the *Confession of Faith*, which appears in Appendix III of this book. These references will be found useful both in counseling and instruction on the religious aspects of marriage.

The United Lutheran Church in America. At the Twentieth Biennial Convention of 1956 the United Lutheran Church adopted the following statement:

Each pastor should require regular counseling periods with couples before marriage. In part this may be done with groups, but private and individual conferences should also be required. [See Appendix IV.]

The United Lutheran Church also at the same Convention adopted a Statement on Marriage and Family Life emphasizing the sacredness of husband-wife relationship and the home as the best channel for Christian nurture, education and evangelization. (*See* Appendix IV.)

The Lutheran Church-Missouri Synod has had a committee in operation since 1947. It has issued an annual parent guidance booklet, *Helping Families through the Church,* and the first of a series of six books in its marriage and family research. The first was entitled *Engagement and Marriage.* The second, not yet published, will deal with the church and sex attitudes. Others will deal with marriage counseling and the field of sex instruction.[9]

The Baptist churches. These churches have no premarital counseling rules binding upon their pastors and have taken no concerted action on the need for such counseling. However, the Christian Life Commission of the Baptist General Convention of Texas has put out a series of leaflets on marriage and family life, and a number of books by Baptist pastors have appeared that should prove helpful to their ministers in premarital counseling.

Space does not permit reviewing the action or lack of it of all the denominations regarding premarital counseling. What I have given is an indication of a fast moving trend in the Church in recognizing the importance of premarital counseling to family life. It is encouraging to note the awakening interest in the preparation of couples for marriage and, correspondingly, the need for ministers to prepare themselves for this vital part of their pastoral duties.

Summary

I wish to emphasize premarital counseling as preventive therapy against sick marriages and divorce. Premarital counseling seeks to help a couple evaluate their relationship before marriage

[9] All of these booklets will be published by the Concordia Press, St. Louis, Mo.

and to acquaint them with ways by which they may build together a happy and successful marriage; or (and this should not be overlooked) to decide against marriage with each other. Clear objective thinking is sought regarding certain areas of difficult adjustment.

Premarital counseling in the Church differs from other counseling in that (1) most couples who come to the minister come at his insistence rather than on their own initiative, and (2) considerable instruction as well as counseling is involved in it.

Couples who come for premarital counseling fall into four groups: (1) emotionally mature individuals, (2) the mismatched, (3) the physically sick or handicapped, and (4) the neurotic or psychotic.

A minimum of eight interviews is recommended: two interviews with the couple together and at least three personal interviews with each partner.

It would be unrealistic to assume that conflicts between happily married spouses do not occur. When two people are joined together in marriage, they bring not only their unique personalities, but, also, their family customs and traditions with them. Many adjustments may be required before smooth teamwork is developed. Premarital counseling helps them evaluate their personality traits and cultural heritages so that when conflicts arise they will not prove fatal to the marriage.

My hypothesis is that premarital counseling should result in a high percentage of happy marriages. My survey, though limited, indicates that the hypothesis is correct.

The Church's responsibility for premarital counseling is being increasingly recognized, as evidenced in various recommendations, resolutions and laws adopted by leading denominations.

METHODS

3

The first interview with the couple

The minister has asked the couple to come and talk with him. This is different from the usual counseling procedure in which the counselee takes the initiative and comes asking for help with some problem. Therefore, the counselor must ask himself many questions. What does this couple expect of me? Now that they are here, just what have I to give them? And how shall I proceed? At what point are they in their courtship? Has everything between them been settled; and are they now just waiting for the wedding date? Most couples are totally unfamiliar with premarital counseling. But most couples do want to make a happy marriage, and want their marriage to last. Therefore, the pastor may assume that they will welcome any help he may have to offer. Sometimes he will meet with resistance, especially from the nonmember of his church, and more often from the man than from the woman.

Let us remember that marriage is an interpersonal relationship. When the pastor sits down with a couple to discuss their relationship in marriage, it is a serious matter. After the marriage, individually they will never again be the same. The interplay of their personalities upon each other will be profound. They may reinforce the best in each other or weaken it. The coming years may change the sweet, smiling, trusting girl into a bitter, resentful, insecure woman, and the handsome, self-confident young man into one of life's failures. So it is a dramatic moment full of promise as well as of uncertainty when the pastor sits down to talk about marriage with two people.

Physical arrangements for counseling

Privacy is essential for good counseling. If the minister holds his interviews in his home study, he should arrange for some sound in the house such as radio or television which will deaden the sound of voices from the study. If the counseling takes place in his office in the church or parish house, precautions should be taken to see that no one may be listening and that voices in the office are softened by rugs, drapes and furniture. The counseling room should be well ventilated, comfortably heated in winter and have a fan or air-conditioning unit in summer.

Comfortable chairs should be provided for the minister and counselee. If the minister is not comfortably seated, he will become tired and restless before the interview is over. It is not easy to sit for an hour to an hour and a half, giving careful attention to what is being said by another. The minister must be relaxed and at ease, but not indifferent. He must remain alert throughout the interview. A comfortable chair helps considerably.

The counselee should also be seated comfortably. A good chair adds dignity to the interview and allows the counselee to relax. A chair with arms enables one to hold on to something while expressing himself forcibly as many will do in counseling sessions. The counselee's chair should face the light which should be properly shaded so as not to be glaring.

There should be no interruptions during the counseling sessions.

A telephone call or a knock on the door may so break a train of thought that it may never be picked up again. If there is a phone in study or office, it should be an extension phone which does not ring. It should be understood by those present in the building that under only emergency circumstances should the minister be interrupted while counseling. Interruptions can spoil a good counseling session.

The minister should prepare to take notes during the interview or write up the case after the interview. Notes enable the counselor to refresh his memory of the interview when he studies the case and is planning for the next interview. A file should be kept in a steel cabinet under lock and key. Only the minister should have a key. It is suggested that when a case is closed or the couple have married, but the file is to be kept for future reference, names should be erased and a code symbol attached to it. This will protect those involved in case of the minister's death; also, in this case, legal arrangements should be made for the destruction of such a file without being read.

I mentioned above a number of items which will add up in expense. If a church understands the minister's work as a counselor, the vestry or official board should be glad to furnish him adequate facilities. Imagine a physician examining his patients in an old room in a parish house without adequate light, heat, chairs, desk or privacy. The minister is just as much a professional as the physician and should insist upon adequate facilities for his work. Most laymen have high regard for the professional man and will regard their minister similarly if their minister expects it. The expense incurred will be amply justified by the results of good counseling.

Early procedure

Before the couple arrive, materials should be in order on the desk. The minister should have these materials ready and know where his procedure leads him, thus reassuring the couple that the pastor is not floundering but knows what he is doing. The following materials are suggested, in order of their use, for the first interview with the couple:

1. *The Marriage Information Blank.* The sample shown contains the necessary information for recording the marriage in the Parish or Church Register. (*See* Appendix V.)

2. *The Schedule for Acquiring Background Information.* (*See* Appendix VI.) The sample shown is of value in obtaining information that will aid in the counseling process. For example, it will give factual information about the couple's similarities or differences in education, an indication of the economic level of their families, and failures in their families to make good marital adjustment, which may in turn affect adjustments in their marriage.

3. *Instruction for the Bride.* This is an outline concerning the conduct of marriages in the local church. It may be mimeographed and contain local regulations such as time and days of weddings; janitor services; use of parish house for reception; fees, such as for the organist; and decorations permitted.

4. *The Declaration of Intention.* This is required to be signed by all couples married by Episcopal ministers. (*See* Appendix VII.) It is preferable that the couple sign the Declaration as printed in the Marriage Service booklet,[1] which contains the Marriage Service, and which is given to the couple following the wedding.

5. The books or pamphlets they are to read which will be given to them at the close of the first interview. For the Methodist couple this would include *In Holy Matrimony, Marriage Manual of the Methodist Church (For Engaged Couples).* It is the official marriage manual of the Methodist church, prepared by directive from the General Conference of 1956 to the General Board of Education.[2]

---

[1] The Marriage Service booklet may be purchased from Moorehouse-Barlow Co., 14 E. 41st St., New York 17, N.Y.

[2] *In Holy Matrimony* may be purchased from The Methodist Publishing House, Nashville, Tenn.

6. A calendar to be used in making the individual appointments.

7. Slips of paper on which to write the appointments.

If all of this material is at hand on the desk, it prevents fumbling and time wasting.

Greeting the couple

The couple should be greeted with friendliness.   This is stressed because usually the man is not of the minister's church and may be quite nervous at meeting the woman's pastor.   His first impression of the pastor may influence his attention toward her church for years to come.   Be pleasant but not pretentious or affected.

People like to be recognized by being called by name.   One's name gives one individuality.   As soon as a good friendly atmosphere has been created, I find it helpful to use first names.

Places to sit should be arranged before the couple arrive.   Point out where they are to sit so there will be no awkwardness.

Reconnaissance information

After a few pleasantries, the couple should be asked to fill out the Marriage Information Blank.

After this has been completed, other information necessary to the interviews should be obtained on the Background Schedule. For this information I prefer "Reconnaissance," used by Sullivan.[3] This information helps the counselor to gain a general view of the individuals and their background.   The Background Schedule is glanced over to determine if it was filled out properly and laid aside temporarily.

The wedding plans

The next subject to be dealt with concerns the wedding plans. If instructions for weddings in the local church have been prepared,

[3] Harry Stack Sullivan, *The Psychiatric Interview* (New York: W. W. Norton & Company, Inc., 1954), p. 72.

printed or mimeographed, they should be given to the couple and explained at this time and coordinated with any plans suggested by the couple.   Even though these plans may have been gone over in detail before by the mother of the bride, it is good to review them briefly with the couple to be sure everyone is agreed on what is to take place and when.   These plans are sometimes so important in the bride's mind that it is useless to try any counseling until they have been gotten out of the way.

Introduction of couple to premarital counseling

We come now to the introduction of the couple to premarital counseling: why and how it is to be done.

The churches are one by one giving statements to their pastors to give them support in their efforts to properly prepare couples for marriage.   Each minister, of course, will use what his own church provides him.   If his church has not yet spoken on the subject, he might read to the couple what other churches have said.   (*See* Appendices.)

Couples are invariably impressed with the Episcopal Church's requirements.   The Episcopal minister should read Canon 17, Sec. 2 (d): "He shall have instructed the parties as to the nature of Holy Matrimony." (*See* Appendix I.)

It is on the strength of this Canon that ministers of the Episcopal Church can insist on the couple's receiving premarital counseling. Many couples do not know about this because some ministers have not informed their people of it, and have not educated the young people to expect it.   The Canon gives the minister a wide range. On the basis of it he can develop his premarital counseling to a fine degree of instruction if he is willing to prepare himself for it.

Canon 17 also requires that "The intention of the parties to contract a marriage shall have been signified to the Minister at least three days before the service of solemnization." Invariably I find that couples are impressed with this time element, not at its length, but the fact that the Episcopal Church does not approve of quick marriages.

The Methodist Church advises that the minister have at least several days' notice before the date of the wedding. Of course, several days is no time at all when it comes to premarital counseling. But it does prevent some hasty marriages and indicates the Church's attitude toward them. The Methodist Church favors legislation requiring a period of days or weeks between the application for a marriage license and the granting of it.

Divorce

Ministers should briefly discuss the problem of divorce with the couple to impress upon them the seriousness of it and how the Church, through premarital counseling is seeking to help her couples make happy and successful marriages.

Most couples quite naturally believe their marriage will be a lasting union. They should realize where their marriage stands statistically and that divorce or lasting friction may occur unless they take safeguards against it.

What are the chances of the success of any marriage? This is a very difficult question to answer. It depends upon the data used in determining the divorce rate in the United States.

Let us take some comparative figures from United States Census Data. In 1930 there were 17.4 divorces per 100 marriages, or 1 divorce per 5.7 marriages; in 1940, 16.5 divorces per 100 marriages or 1 divorce per 6 marriages. But in 1946, the first year after World War II when the effect of war marriages, often hasty ones, began to be felt, there were 26.6 divorces per 100 marriages, or 1 divorce per 3.8 marriages. By 1950 the ratio of marriages and divorces had come more into line with the gradual incline shown for past decades: 23.0 divorces per 100 marriages or 1 divorce per 4.3 marriages. Baber draws the conclusion[4] that a marriage (first

[4] Roy E. Baber, *Marriage and the Family* (New York: McGraw-Hill Book Company, Inc., © 1953), p. 450.

marriages and remarriages combined) faces a 25 per cent probability of divorce. He would give first marriages a slightly smaller risk, and feels that this 1 in 4 rate may underestimate their chances of success.

Divorce not necessarily the solution to personality problems

Premarital counseling should emphasize this probability of divorce, and the couple should be helped to understand that divorce is not always the solution to their personality problems which may underlie unhappiness in marriage. In fact, many divorced persons form a second or third union with no improvement in the marriage relationship. Divorce seldom solves the basic problem.[5] And the effect of the divorce upon the individuals involved may be very disastrous. Couples who receive premarital counseling should learn from it that there are agencies and professionally trained individuals to help them find solutions to problems arising in marriage and to correct maladjustments which may develop.

There are some who feel that marriage can be safeguarded by making divorce illegal. Personally, I do not believe we can legislate people into satisfactory relationships and into staying happily married. Legislation cannot make an unhappy marriage happy. It cannot create love between two people who are basically incompatible. Divorce can best be decreased by education for marriage and parenthood, and especially by teaching the spiritual and moral basis for each.

A basis for solving marital problems

A marriage which is well rooted in the Church, with both husband and wife taking their spiritual life seriously, offers a basis for solving marital problems and living together happily in a permanent union.

[5] See Landis and Landis, *Building a Successful Marriage,* 3rd ed., pp. 6-7 and Bergler, *Unhappy Marriage and Divorce,* p. 11.

"The big problem is not to keep people who want divorce from getting it, but to keep more people from wanting divorce." [6] This means we must provide adequate premarital counseling for our young people and skilled counseling for those who are faced with grave marital problems which threaten the permanence of the marriage.

Most marriages are already broken when they reach the divorce court so that the divorce merely recognizes that the marriage no longer exists. Some who feel that marriage is indissoluble quote the scripture, "Those whom God has joined together let no man put asunder," but it is hard to believe that God has had anything at all to do with some marriages. They were not based on love, no inner union ever took place, no sacrament worthy of the name was created.

The Church is not interested in the contracting of such marriages. It is interested primarily in Christian marriages and the establishment of Christian homes; and, secondarily, in all marriages because the home is the primary and basic social institution.

The Church's primary interest

It comes as a surprise to some couples when told that the Church is interested primarily in Christian marriages, and that since they have come to a minister for the blessing of their marriage the Church assumes that they want to build a Christian home.

Now, at this point following the discussion of divorce, the couple might be asked to discuss what they consider are the essential elements that make up a Christian home and some of the causes for divorce they have heard of from friends—especially friends who have been through divorce.

To quote Baber:

Marriage would be immeasurably strengthened, and the frequency of divorce correspondingly reduced, if couples would thoughtfully and honestly work out their philosophy of marriage before they embark,

[6] Baber, *Marriage and the Family,* p. 527.

deciding what they can reasonably expect from it and what they cannot; how much failure they can have in some lesser aspects of it without losing the greater, basic values, which inevitably would bring collapse. A young married couple often fear that any little scratch on furniture or wall of their new home will ruin it, but as the years pass, they find that it can take a good deal of buffeting and still remain very attractive and comfortable. So do they learn that their marriage is not ruined by minor dents and markings, for it is sturdy enough to stand the buffeting of differences of opinion and occasional quarrels and still remain a secure and comfortable abode of love and satisfying companionship.

But the rising spirit of individualism makes many a person entering matrimony unwilling to formulate a reasonable philosophy of marriage and prevents him from living up to it even if once formulated. The utter self-centeredness, which so often shows up on the fading afterglow of the honeymoon, soon creates an intolerable situation for one or both, as is shown by the fact that the highest incidence of divorce is in the second year of marriage. Such raw egoism regards divorce as the way to avoid making any concessions. It is, as one writer puts it, "an orgy of the ego, . . . an indulgence of the gratification of the immediate desires of man or wife without regard to family, children, or state." It is "individualism gone mad." [7]

Lack of preparation for marriage

People seem to prepare for everything except marriage. A homely comparison may illustrate a point here. A friend of ours raises black angus cattle. He told me that before he dared put any money in cattle he studied cattle raising and the peculiarities of black angus for three years. But how many couples spend any time at all preparing to "raise" a family! The writer is very much pleased that more and more of our schools and colleges are providing courses in home economics, child training, family life, and human relations. In my opinion the family is of such great importance to church and state that courses for men and women in one or more of these fields should be required. Individuals who

[7] *Ibid.,* p. 492.

have had such courses are invariably interested in receiving premarital counseling. Although the time is short with many couples, the Church through premarital counseling can help her young people build their marriages on more secure and solid foundations than they might otherwise, and emphasize the need for the study of child training before their children are born.

Marriage has the best chance of succeeding where there has been adequate preparation for it—physical, psychological, and spiritual. One major cause of divorce would seem to be the lack of preparation for marriage.

Introducing the Declaration of Intention

Much more can be said about the Church's interest in marriage and the homes of her people, but it is leading up to "The Declaration of Intention," required by the Episcopal Church to be signed before the solemnization of the marriage. (*See* Appendix VII.) Ministers of other churches will naturally use whatever those churches may require. "The Declaration of Intention" may, however, be used by any minister-counselor as a guide for the first interview with the couple. "The Declaration," along with other requirements of the Episcopal Church, is presented in this manual as illustrative material to ministers of other churches.

Very few people know about "The Declaration of Intention." In fact in a survey made in 1957 of couples married in the Episcopal Churches in one of our large cities it was found that only about 50 per cent recalled having heard of or signed "The Declaration."

Those clergy who have it signed merely as a Canonical requirement are failing to use beneficially one of the best ready-made instruments put into their hands. It is so broad and thorough that it can be made the basis of an entire series of counseling sessions depending on the imagination and ingenuity of the minister.

Preferring to use the Marriage Service Book which has the Declaration in the front, the author gives this to the couple and reads it over to them. Then it is discussed item by item.

The Trinitarian Formula

The form in the Canon does not have the heading "In the name of the Father, and of the Son, and of the Holy Ghost. Amen." The one in the Marriage Service Book does have it.

The Trinitarian Formula lifts marriage to the very highest level. It gives a deep religious direction to everything that follows. The mutual love, esteem, cooperation, and justice exemplified in the relationship between the Persons of the Trinity set the ideal for a Christian marriage. No person is sufficient unto himself. In marriage this is emphasized as husband and wife complete their sufficiency in each other and their children. Even as the triune God finds his completeness not in self-sufficiency but in out-going love.

Christian marriage defined

The Declaration suggests a definition of Christian marriage which may be taken as a corollary to our definition in Chapter 1.

Christian marriage is a life-long union of husband and wife with a complete sharing of body, mind, and spirit; for the purpose of mutual fellowship, encouragement and understanding; for the procreation (if it may be) of children, and their physical and spiritual nurture; for the safeguarding and benefit of society.

Two essential components of Christian marriage

Christian marriage implies first of all two Christian people as its necessary components. Here the counselor may inquire of both parties what may be their church interests. If one party is not a church member, he or she may be interested in discussing at some other time with the minister the matter of baptism. Usually the non-Christian party is quite willing to do this and indeed may welcome the opportunity and later request baptism before the marriage. In some cases this preparation for baptism may require more time than the premarital counseling, but it gives the minister a rare opportunity to relate the redeeming power of Christ to the whole of life and especially to the role of spouse and parent.

A *life-long union*

Young people sometimes say of marriage that "if it doesn't work out, we can always get a divorce" or "marriage is a gamble." Those who enter marriage with such hidden provisions have not yet made a total commitment to contract a Christian marriage. They have not analyzed the depth of Christian love in which their marriage must be rooted. The counselor might challenge the couple to think about their love in terms of a life-long union which is sure to run into the usual storms and stresses of life which may at times severely test the bonds of matrimony. Whether those bonds will hold or not will depend in part upon the quality of the love which cements them. Of course, there are those who will accept marriage and its indissolubility on an intellectual basis and remain together not because they love each other but because they do not believe in divorce. There are others who will remain partners to a marriage because of the protection it gives them in the extra-marital relationships. And there are still others who will stay within a marriage because of the security found in the family as an institution.

A woman of about 38 consulted me about her marriage which was about to end in divorce. She had one child. In seeking to determine what lay behind the difficulty with her marriage, I was told that she married not for love—though she hoped that would develop—but because she was nearing 30, wanted security and an escape from an unhappy home situation, and was afraid this man might be her last chance. Of course, there are men who marry because they want to experience again the security of their childhood home and mother. All of these people may indeed form life-long unions as husband and wife, technically speaking, but without experiencing the emotional satisfaction found in a happy and successful marriage based upon Christian love.

The main objective of premarital counseling by the minister

Premarital counseling by a minister should help lay the foundation for a happy and successful marriage within the framework of Christian faith. All through the interviews this objective should be highlighted. Herein lies the value of the minister's counseling in contrast to the professional or secular counselor. This concerns Christian marriages which are to be solemnized in the Church according to the Church's teaching and liturgy.

Marriage and matrimony

Some couples look upon a wedding as a social affair primarily. It might be helpful to distinguish between marriage, "the institution whereby men and women are joined in a special kind of social and legal dependence, for the purpose of founding and maintaining a family," [8] and matrimony, "the rite and act of marrying" [9] which is described in the Church as "Holy Matrimony" and is quite explicitly a religious affair.

It must be emphasized that although the marriage ceremony involves social activities, the usual parties and reception with the rice throwing, old shoes, and whatnot have their place in making the marriage a very joyous occasion. The primary function from the Church's standpoint is the joining together of the man and woman in Christian wedlock in the presence of God and before the representatives of the Church. And those who ask for the Church's blessing upon their marriage must come to this sacred service "reverently, discretely, advisedly, soberly and in the fear of God." [10]

---

[8] By permission. From *Webster's New International Dictionary*, 2nd ed., © 1959 by G. & C. Merriam Co., Publishers of the Merriam-Webster Dictionaries.
[9] *Ibid.*
[10] *Book of Common Prayer*, p. 300.

Characteristics of a happy marriage

Sharing. If a Christian marriage is anything at all, it is a sharing between a man and a woman of their whole selves, which may be described in terms of communication. It is based upon mutual trust implying a willingness to give themselves completely and unreservedly to each other. "But is this not capitulation?" a young woman asked. No, it is not capitulation, because that implies that one party does all the giving, whereas in complete sharing in marriage each tries to outdo the other.

I have indicated in my definition three areas of sharing: body, mind, and spirit. In discussing these I do not go into too much detail at this point, because these areas will come up again in the personal interviews. However, this is a good place to explain to both parties the general ideas involved in mutual sharing such as communication and empathy.

Communication. Nothing can really take place between individuals unless there is communication between them. It is through communication that each spouse shares his or her real self and real attitudes with the other, resulting in the experience of giving and receiving love in a trusting, understanding interpersonal relationship. Likewise, when communication breaks down between a husband and wife, the marital relationship deteriorates rapidly.

Communication takes place in many ways: verbally, by gestures, glances, physical closeness. Almost every show of recognition between two individuals is communication of a kind and may be friendly or hostile. When a man and woman say "There is no longer any communication between us," they mean usually that a kind of barrier has risen between them. They are no longer in tune. The lines of communication have broken down.

Now, communication does not depend on words. Take for example a baby and his mother. Communication is present as soon as the mother holds the baby for the first time. Something indefinable seems to flow between them along with the mother's milk.

The warmth of the baby, its cuddling, its cooing, its satisfied kicking, clutching, all convey something to the mother that awakens in her deep maternal feelings: desires to love, protect, and nourish the child. While we cannot ask the baby to describe his feelings, we do know that babies seem to sense when they are loved and secure. An atmosphere of quarreling can produce colic or a skin rash; rejection by the mother has a similar effect. Wherever there is deep love between two people, there is this sort of communication between them. They "feel" when the other is happy or anxious or relaxed in peace.

Empathy. Communication is linked with empathy, which is the ability to understand the feelings and motives of another. Often what one says is not what one means, nor does it express what one feels. Behind words and gestures there are sometimes hidden motives to which those whom we love can respond only if they are sensitive to the deep emotions of the other one. Couples need to know how important it is that each spouse knows how to enter into the feelings of the other. This is not sympathy. Empathy is the ability to see things from the other's frame of reference, to see the world as the other sees it, and perhaps most important of all, to see the other spouse as that one sees himself. It is feeling into the emotions of the other and perceiving problems as the other perceives them. This demands objectivity so that one does not interpret the activities of the other subjectively, but is able to trust the other's love, even when external facts may seem to the contrary.

A young wife was almost on the point of dissolving her marriage because her husband had entered upon a business contract without first telling her about it. She felt it indicated a lack of love on his part. Actually, this had never occurred to him. An opportunity presented itself, he took advantage of it, and told his wife later. He also showed a lack of empathy toward his wife in not perceiving her need to know about his plans and in not keeping her informed. Lack of empathic understanding on the part of both came close to spoiling a very good marriage. For a while a barrier stood between them. There was no communication. But there was a strong love at the basis of their marriage, and communication was soon restored as the feelings and motives of each were recognized.

Husbands and wives who truly love each other find many ways to communicate. In fact, everything they do together becomes a communication of their love and feeling toward each other.

Three areas of sharing

Body. This brings us to the question of physical sharing. Marriage involves a complete sharing of the body. Of course, this refers to the physical aspects of marriage—specifically to sex in marriage. The subject is never taken up in this first interview with the couple, because some are not comfortable in the discussion of sex, especially with the other partner to the marriage present. I merely mention here that the complete sharing of the body is, of course, a very important part of marriage and that we shall take it up later. (*See* Chapter 9.) In this connection the couple should be urged to have a physical examination. In some states this is required before the marriage license can be issued. The reasons for a physical examination should be explained: to be certain one is free of communicable disease; that the woman's internal organs are in position for conception; that intercourse may be had without pain to the woman; that both will be assured that they contribute to the union a sound and healthy body.

Mind. Marriage is also a complete sharing of the mind or intellect. Communication so often breaks down here. A common complaint in unhappy marriages is that one of the partners does not share intellectually with the other. There are no exchange of ideas and no mental stimulation in the marriage, resulting in boredom. Each one should share his reading, political thinking, social concepts, ideas for oneself as well as for the marriage, and all the other things which the mind is able to encompass.

Some couples are a great stimulation to each other because of their keen and active minds. One of the tragedies of American education is the failure to help our young people plan future study programs after high school and college. One need only to observe the sparse libraries in the homes of our average families. A family should be proud of its intellectual accomplishments and cultural advantages it can offer its members. Perhaps our failure here is due to our rather limited conception of what constitutes an education. Many of our young people learn in school and college only to endure the accumulation of knowledge without any conception of its use. It never becomes integrated into the personality of some individuals.

A very intellectual couple, each with a Ph.D. degree, was on the point of separating. One of the complaints of the wife was that her husband never shared himself with her intellectually. He held himself aloof and superior to her. She often brought up matters of government, economics, or community projects and would seek to discuss them with him. But he never had any contribution to make. There was little left except the physical union to hold this marriage together.

Television provides an ideal escape within the home for the person who is not very communicative or who has a tendency toward withdrawal. The complaints are common in which a spouse criticizes the other for sitting through evening after evening looking at television, thus cutting off communication between them. Wives make this complaint more frequently than husbands, who are accused of coming home after work to fall into a routine of eating supper, looking at television, and going to bed. In this way the husband builds a wall around himself as effective as a barrier of stone. One young attractive wife was so infuriated by this behavior that in her frustration she began screaming at her husband and threatened to leave. In counseling, she wept saying, "There is no sharing between us of anything of common interest. I want to talk about our home, our plans for children, the things I read, but he won't do anything but sit by the hour glued to television." In premarital counseling couples should be made aware of those pleasure-interests such as television, radio, or reading which can gradually become methods of escape from facing problems of marital adjustments, which reinforce a tendency toward withdrawal and shyness, or even of intellectual shallowness which might be partly corrected by the wholesome sharing of minds.

Heart. There must be a sharing of the heart or emotion. Husbands and wives should be able to spill over to each other, knowing that each will be understood by the other. This emotional sharing based upon mutual love and esteem is one of the finest qualities in a happy marriage. It enables husband and wife to participate together in life's dramatic moments and to meet crises jointly, to strengthen each other in the change of direction every crisis brings about, so that the new course may be pursued courageously and creatively.

Empathy and sharing of emotions are closely related. Sometimes we are unable to share in the emotions of another because we interpret subjectively the situations presented. Let me illustrate. A young wife greeted her husband joyfully, exclaiming that she was pregnant. But the husband's reaction was anything but empathic. He replied, "Oh! No! Not now. I've got to get my degree." He perceived the whole situation as an obstacle to his studies and made his wife feel that she was to blame. What might have been a wonderful memory of mutual joy ended up in accusations and unhappiness.

A man whose wife had described him as lacking in self-confidence came home one evening highly elated because friends had urged him to run for a public office. He wanted most of all to share this with his wife. But when he told her, she replied, "You don't want that office. You have all you can do in your business. Tell them you don't want to run." The man was so deflated by this lack of empathic understanding that he made further political plans without his wife's knowledge until it was settled that he would run. He ran and was elected. His wife interpreted this subjectively, saying that he showed no consideration for her. It is very important that couples understand each other's needs, desires, and aims in life, so that they can share in the emotional crises that arise and understand the difference between subjective and objective interpretation of situations and events.

Habitual behavior

In order to help one understand his own reactions in crises, it is necessary to ask how he has handled emotional upsets in the past: did he run and hide or cry or sulk or hit aimlessly whatever was near, striking out with fist or with words? Or did he learn to talk over his emotional upsets, taking hold of the crisis constructively in order to work through to some solution of the problem? Remember, in a crisis a person generally reverts to a juvenile level of behavior. It is important to know whether or not that is the way in which a person meets his crises. When two people get upset, each upsets the other, and soon both are screaming at each other. Good counseling before marriage could have helped them to correct such immature behavior.

This was true of Jack and Sue. In the premarital counseling, Jack told about how childishly he reacted to various little crises, such as losing at tennis. He became angry so that the two seemed to be fussing all the time, and he thought seriously of calling off their marriage. When each recognized that his behavior patterns were immature and saw himself objectively, each learned to help the other in a crisis by not reacting with the same childish pattern of behavior, but by maintaining the role of a mature person. It is certain that a person who is relieved of these immature patterns of behavior will develop a productive personality. These juvenile patterns of behavior which all of us bring over into adulthood are among the main causes for maladjustment and failure in marriage.

Use of mental health principles

We have opportunity here to point out the need for developing good mental health as a basis for building a happy marriage. A good supply of mental health literature should be kept on hand for use of couples.[10]

The next step: the Declaration and mutuality

The second paragraph of the Declaration of Intention—the next phrase in the definition of marriage—states: "We believe it is for the purpose of mutual fellowship, encouragement, and understanding."

Fellowship. The meaning of mutual fellowship is fairly obvious. The more things a couple enjoys together, the closer will be their relationship and the happier they will be. It is well to ask a couple to name their mutual interests. Sometimes there will be a sparsity of interests. Some may have shared no interests except the drive-in theatre where they could "pet" unobserved and undisturbed. Other couples will list a variety of interests. Those whose mutual interests are limited will find it difficult to enrich their fellowship together. They should be encouraged to develop mutual interests before marriage.

People who really love each other can cultivate each other's interests. A well-known movie actress said on a television interview that when she married, her husband liked fishing and she liked bridge. So in order that they might be together more, she learned to fish and he learned to play bridge. A girl whose husband was an amateur radio fan, who talked radio "all day long," decided to study radio also, so that she could share his hobby with him. A city girl married a man who loved outdoor life, camping, hunting and fishing. She determined to cultivate a taste of the out-of-doors, and together they have camped in America's most renowned scenic spots. Couples should go over their mutual interests and plan to maintain an interest in each other's hobbies, pleasures, and recreational activities.

Encouragement. There is nothing more wholesome than a man

[10] For this purpose, *see Public Affairs Pamphlets.* For list and prices write to: Public Affairs Committee, 22 East 38th Street, New York 1, N.Y.

and wife encouraging each other to exploit his or her finest and strongest potentialities. Everyone has some capabilities which need to be developed and enhanced. Freud speaks of love and work as essential to true happiness. A man who leaves home in the morning in the full assurance of his wife's love and dependence on him and admiration of him as a man will work hard and happily through the day inspired by the expectation of her welcoming smile and the warmth of her embrace when he returns in the evening. The wife who remains at home to keep house and to care for the children will go about her duties with a sparkle in her eyes, a song on her lips, and joy in her heart knowing that her man is dependent on her for love and is using his energies through the day for the security of the home.

As the husband's mind turns back many times during the day to his wife and home, eager to return, her thoughts follow him in his work as she happily anticipates his returning home at dusk. This is the way the Christian couple should be thinking while absent from each other during the day. The going out in the morning and the coming in at night for every member of the family should be happy occasions without bickering and nagging. Nowadays, when a husband and wife leave together each morning for their jobs, it is all the more important that each knows and accepts his role in the family and parts eager to return to each other and to home when the day's work is over. True love inspires one to work; and to work for the object of one's love is not really "work" but joy in accomplishment.

Understanding. Understanding is a word everyone needs to know better. Literally, it means to stand under so as to grasp completely the meaning, the feelings, the intentions of another with the aim of assisting, helping, responding to the needs of the other. Where there is mutual understanding between husband and wife, each will feel comfortable with the other. Each will wish that he or she be understood, even when in error. It involves perception of the feelings of the other person—that which is also called empathy or "feeling into" another.

Three pillars of a happy marriage

Preston says that mental health rests upon three pillars: affection, praise, and consistency.[11] The same is true of a happy and successful marriage, for that is the kind of marriage mentally healthy people should make. The author would add appreciation to praise. Nothing encourages one more than affection and appreciation.

Affection. Most people like affection. Even those who say that they are not affectionate really mean that they have never learned how to receive and give affection. The need for affection is innate. Studies made of institutionalized infants revealed that despite proper diet and care the mortality rate was high. But when "foster mothers" were employed to come each day to massage and mother the babies, the mortality rate declined. Those infants who survived without this care showed general inability to adjust socially. As one investigator expressed it: "Those who died suffered a gradual breakdown under stress, beginning with loss of appetite and sleeplessness, and ending with inability to withstand even minor ailments. Love-starved, they were crippled in the battle for life." [12]

In a study of infantile experience in relation to personality development, Ribble found that inadequate "mothering" of infants produced either a form of negativistic excitement or a form of regressive quiescence. Here, again, the introduction of a "foster mother" to give personal care and to massage these infants, thereby showing affection for them, brought dramatic results in restoring appetite, alertness and reflex excitability.[13]

It is not enough to give gifts as signs of affection. Affection must be demonstrated in overt acts toward the loved one: kissing, embracing, holding hands, caressing, saying in words, "I love you," and repeating other endearing terms are the usual ways we show

---

[11] George H. Preston, M.D., *The Substance of Mental Health* (New York: Rinehart and Company, Inc., 1943), p. 132.

[12] Rene A. Spitz, "Milk and Love," *Time*, May 5, 1952, p. 51.

[13] Adapted from Margaret A. Ribble, "Infantile Experience in Relation to Personality Development" in *Personality and the Behavior Disorders*, ed. J. McV. Hunt, p. 621. © 1944, The Ronald Press Company.

affection in our American culture. And since this is our culture, husband and wife expect rightfully these demonstrations of affection.

Will and Jane had not kissed each other for several years. He left for work in the morning without even a "good bye" and when he came in at night he grunted, sat down to read the paper, ate, and went to bed. Yet, the two said they loved each other in spite of some quarrelling. Neither seemed able to break through the psychological impasse in affection. Finally, the wife decided she would take the initiative and kiss her husband when he came home from work. She did. Her report was "He liked it!" The barrier was overcome, affection wrapped them together once more in love and esteem.

A young woman in premarital counseling said that she had never seen her mother and father kiss each other. Her fiance complained that she was not affectionate, whereas he was. He was wondering how their marriage would succeed. The girl had, of course, no pattern to follow. She had never learned to show affection. In premarital counseling the need for affection in the family relationship was discussed, both her need to demonstrate by affectionate acts her love for her husband and his need for her affection, as well as her own need for his affection. But it was not easy for her now to bring into the marriage relationship something she had never experienced as a child and had sealed off from her conscious behavior toward her father. Her fiance tried to help her with this problem, but received little response. Years later we learned the marriage was shaky because of the man's excessive drinking and abuse of his wife. We can only wonder if she never learned to be affectionate and if that was contributory to his drinking problem.

Appreciation. Along with affection goes appreciation. Everyone wants to be thought well of by the significant love figure in his life. A wife who tries to prod her husband to success by criticizing him, or comparing him to affluent neighbors, can soon so undermine his self-confidence that he will fail instead of succeed.

Every normal wife wants her husband to get ahead. She wants to be proud of him, to look up to him. And she wants to feel that she had some share in his rise in the world.

Jack was a broken man at 29 when he came for counseling. With his head in his hands, he could only say over and over, "I'm a failure." He had a college education. He was a professional man who should have been well on his way to success. "You say that you are a failure?" "My wife has been telling me that for the past three years. She asks over and over, 'Why don't I make the salary Ed makes? Why don't we have a car like the Smiths?' I can't get ahead. My income gets less and less. My heart's not in my work." The wife also came for counseling. I suggested that she use better tactics on her husband: that she never again call him a failure or compare him unfavorably to anyone else; but that she begin to praise him for any and every thing that he did well, and show her appreciation of him as a husband. She agreed to do this and to display a lot of love and affection. The effect upon her husband was little short of miraculous. Interest in his work returned. Relations with his friends and clients improved. His income improved. About a year or so later he came by to tell us that he was out of debt.

An appropriate illustration of appreciation was given in a book on happiness: On the tombstone of her husband's grave, a southern mountain woman had chiseled in rough and uneven letters this epitaph: "He always appreciated." [14]

A wise husband will let his wife know that he appreciates her cooking, housework, care of the children and love-making. He will praise her and show his pride in her accomplishments, and she in his.

Consistency. But in all of this, one must be consistent. A man once said to me about his wife, "I would rather have her mean all the time, than loving one day and mean the next. When I

[14] Albert Edward Wiggam, *New Techniques of Happiness* (New York: Wilfred Funk, Inc., 1948), p. 307.

leave home in the morning I never know what kind of reception I will receive when I return at night. Living with her as she is is enough to drive me mad."

Here is a good place to ask the couples about their moods. One may say that he is grouchy before breakfast; another that he must have a cup of coffee to get going. Again one may have periods of depression when he wants to be left alone. These moods can be quite changeable, and may be exhibited in various ways: cutting remarks, tearfulness, quick anger, sulking. This interview with the couple is not the time to go into these moods, but merely to get some expression of them in the other's presence, as an aid toward objectivity. An analysis of the moods and their origin should follow in the personal interviews. Only a note of them is made now.

It is not easy to live with a moody person. He cannot be consistent in dealing with affection and appreciation. Every incident is colored by his mood. A husband, returning home with good news about a promotion, may have cold water dashed in his face by a moody wife who happens at that moment to be consumed with self-pity. Moodiness is evidence of immaturity, lack of objectivity and control over one's emotions.

So we have these three pillars of good mental health for a happy marriage: affection, appreciation and consistency. They can bring much encouragement to husband and wife as each one uses them as expressions of love of the other.

Spouses should be good listeners

Husbands and wives should learn to be good listeners to each other's problems without arguing or attempting to refute the other's declarations of what may have happened during the day. Each should create a permissive atmosphere in which each may unburden verbally the exasperations, disappointments, discouragements, as well as successes, accomplishments and joys of the day, feeling that his own disappointments and pleasures are accepted and understood as a part of one's whole self.

This was expressed by a man who said that when he came home, whatever he tried to tell his wife was picked to pieces and "she divides me up instead of taking me as a whole person. I know that I have weaknesses and I know that I have good points. She overlooks the good and magnifies the bad. Why can't she accept me whole?"

Everyone wants to be understood as a whole person and not analyzed in pieces. An understanding wife or husband should know this.

Many a husband would have escaped stomach ulcers from worry and anxiety if he had had an understanding wife to whom he could have turned as a therapist and ventilated his fears and anxieties, without the fear of being scolded, lectured, laughed at or having to enter into a debate. And, of course, the same applies vice-versa to the wife.

Sometimes husbands think their wife's household problems or relations with neighbors are trivial. But nothing that incurs anxiety is trivial to the individual. Empathy is the ability to perceive reality as the other person perceives it, or to see "the world of experience as nearly as possible through his eyes." [15]

Through understanding, husbands and wives can enable each other to get relief from much of the pressure of modern life.

A simple formula for a happy marriage

Marriage is never a one-way proposition, but mutual relationship throughout. Selfishness simply has no place in marriage. The author's simple formula for a happy marriage is never consciously to do anything one knows is displeasing to the other partner, and to do everything one knows is pleasing to the other partner. This

[15] Carl R. Rogers, *Client Centered Therapy* (Boston: Houghton Mifflin Company, 1951), p. 494.

formula will cover acts of courtesy, consideration, and kindness. It moves oneself to the background and the other person into the foreground: evidence of maturity and Christian living at its best. When two people strive to live together on that basis, friction will be at a minimum. Indeed, to put that formula to work is to open the way for the exciting exploration of love for the greatest benefit of the family.

Parental responsibility and planned parenthood

Children are a great blessing to every marriage and form a strong bond between husband and wife. Couples should plan intelligently for children. Planned parenthood [16] is as much a part of God's guiding today, as is any other of our discoveries which enable us to live more wholesome and happier lives. Many couples discuss having children and methods of birth control before marriage. God gave us intelligence and He intends for us to use it in properly spacing children. A young couple has many adjustments to make and should have time to get to know one another without having to face the immediacy of pregnancy, especially in the case of the very young, those with short acquaintance, and those compulsive about getting married. Premarital counseling should help such couples especially to appreciate the wisdom of planned parenthood. But, if a mature couple desires children soon after marriage and has no particular reason for postponing pregnancy, we would agree that they should let nature take her course, which position is in keeping with the teaching of the churches. In any event the couple should realize that today with our new knowledge about birth control, the freedom of choice is theirs.

However, in Christian marriage a couple's choice should be made prayerfully and in the light of Christian teaching. The Protestant churches in general seem to approve of planned parenthood. The Methodist Church states: "We believe that planned

[16] For further information, write to Planned Parenthood Federation of America, Inc., 301 Madison Ave., New York 22, N.Y.

Parenthood, practiced in Christian conscience, may fulfill rather than violate the will of God." (*See* Appendix II.) The Committee on the Family in Contemporary Society of the Lambeth Conference 1958 says:

It must be emphasized once again that family planning ought to be the result of thoughtful and prayerful Christian decision. Where it is, Christian husbands and wives need feel no hesitation in offering their decision humbly to God and following it with a clear conscience. The means of family planning are in large measure matters of clinical and aesthetic choice, subject to the requirement that they be admissible to the Christian conscience. Scientific studies can rightly help, and do, in assessing the effects and the usefulness of any particular means; and Christians have every right to use the gifts of science for proper ends. [*See* Appendix I.]

The methods of birth control are better taken up with the couple individually when sex in marriage is discussed. This might be done by a physician, if allowed legally.

The safeguard and benefit of society

In discussing the next phrase, "for the safeguard and benefit of society," the minister has an opportunity to help the couple see their home in the larger framework of the social order, and their responsibility to establish a home that will be an asset to the community. There are many homes that take from the community all that they can get: education, religious instruction, and ministrations, various communal benefits such as police protection, and sanitation, but never put anything into the community life. They participate in no community activities. They are interested only in what the community can give to them, with no thought of their responsibility to give to the community. A young couple who establishes a home and immediately begins to share their talents with the community will win the love and esteem of their fellow citizens and make the community a better place for all.

God's help essential to a Christian marriage

By the time the minister has guided a couple through the first interview to this point, and having encompassed the main ideas in the Declaration of Intention, or the definition of a Christian marriage, they come now to the last and most important: "And we do engage ourselves, so far as in us lies, to make our utmost effort to establish this relationship and to seek God's help thereto."

Marriage, like any other undertaking, will succeed or fail according to the time, effort and thought put into it. A couple must work at the marriage constantly if it is to succeed. Romance must be kept alive. Each must continue to do the little things, little surprises, that were done to win each other before marriage. Romance adds zest and thrills to marriage even more perhaps than it did to the courtship.

Romantic attitudes, holding over from the engagement period, aid in the early adjustments of husband and wife. They still perceive each other through rose-tinted glasses and respond to the image which each has constructed of the other. The courtship tendency of each to "put one's best foot forward" continues. In many marriages romantic attitudes and the idealization of the other persist long after marriage and in some cases throughout life. Romantic love functions to facilitate the day-by-day adjustments necessary for the success of marriage.[17]

The Christian couple will seek God's help in their effort to establish the kind of relationship we have been discussing. The minister will have many suggestions for this: church attendance, family prayer and personal prayer. Since the marriage begins at God's Altar it should be kept there by regular worship. God instituted marriage, and no one is more concerned for the success of a marriage than God and His Church.

The Methodist Church has adopted the following Resolution on the Christian Family:

[17] Ernest Burgess and Harvey J. Locke, *The Family* (New York: American Book Company, Inc., 1945), p. 580.

The modern family is struggling against great difficulties: the tensions created by the world situation, uncertainties due to the present military demands on youth, inadequate housing, uprooting of families due to unprecedented population shifts, and the coarsening influence of many mass media on the lives of children.   The end result of these difficulties is evidenced by the high rate of divorce, juvenile delinquency, broken lives, and a general laxity of moral standards.   It is only when the family fulfills its highest functions and is truly Christian that its members rise above these difficulties and thus aid in halting the trends threatening the home.

The home is the place where emotional weaknesses of the members of the family come to light, where children express their innate hunger to be secure, to belong, to be needed, to be recognized.

Religion and the family naturally belong together.   What religion is to accomplish it can do best in the family.   What the family must do, it cannot do without religion.   Religion and the family are natural allies.   Religion is inseparable from the family.   Family life at its best is a matter of living life at the deepest level, which is a level of relationship to God.

1.   *What Is a Christian Family?*—A Christian family is one in which parents so live the Christian life and practice the presence of God that children come to accept God as the greatest reality of life.

A Christian family is one in which each member is accepted and respected as a person having sacred worth.

A Christian family is one that seeks to bring every member into the Christian way of living.

A Christian family is one that accepts the responsibility of worship and instruction to the end of developing the spiritual life of each person.

A Christian family is one that manifests a faith in God, observes daily prayer and grace at meals, is committed to behavior in keeping with Christian ideals for family relations, community life, and national and world citizenship.   [*See* Appendix II.]

Closing the interview

After the discussion, the couple may be asked if they wish to sign the Declaration then or later.   Generally, they wish to sign immediately.

The couple should be reminded again to have a good physical examination by their doctor. For the woman, this should include a gynecological examination.

The books selected should be given to them and both should be asked to read them before the marriage.

The last thing to do is to arrange for at least three appointments for each one and a final appointment for the couple together.

The interview may be closed with a prayer.

After the couple has gone

After the couple has gone is a good time for the pastor to make a few notes on his impression of them as a couple entering matrimony. How do they complement each other? What about the psychological distance between them? Which one seems to dominate? Do they seem to be cooperative, or do they pull against each other?

A good deal of information should have been gathered which now must be used as reconnaissance material for the individual interviews. Of course, much more information will be gained in these interviews so that by the time the couple comes back together for their final interview, the counselor will have a firm basis for seeing that either a strong foundation will have been laid for a successful marriage, or it will have become clear to him and the couple that they are either unsuited or unready for each other without further preparation or should give up the marriage.

Summary

Premarital counseling is such a new field that the minister will find in it recurring freshness and a real source of imagination as he introduces it to each couple. More and more he will come to realize the inadequacy of divorce in solving personal problems and the possibilities in premarital counseling as a way to decrease the incidence of unhappy marriage and divorce.

The Church's interest is in the formation of Christian homes. Several churches have placed their ministers in a strong position by Canons and statements which require them to give instruction in Christian marriage. The Declaration of Intention used in the Episcopal Church establishes a basis and outline for it. In this chapter we have attempted to indicate to the minister-counselor, without much detail, how this Declaration may be used. Each minister will develop his own methods and techniques according to his interest in this field and degree of study and preparation for counseling.

4

The personal interviews

In the first personal interview, Adele came right to the point by saying, "I am not at all sure that this will be the marriage I want. The whole problem is that John is so dependent on his parents. He is an only child and spoiled. He turns to his parents for everything, and they give anything he asks for. I have been on my own since my father died when I was twelve. I have lived with my grandmother, or off at school. I'm very independent. John is just the opposite." Here was a problem that could not be dealt with in one or two interviews. It took several before both of them (for he, too, had doubts) felt that they had worked through to an understanding of the other's needs. We were also able to get his parents to come for an interview, resulting in quite a change in attitude on their part which enabled the young couple to make a good adjustment in their marriage.

As already indicated, there will be required at least three personal interviews with each party. From the above illustration we see one typical beginning of the personal interviews. Not all interviews begin as Adele's did, but if the first interview with the couple went off well—that is, if they understood the purpose of premarital counseling and how it can help them toward an understanding of each other so that their marriage may be a happy one, then one or both of them may quite readily come into the first personal interview with a problem that is of real concern to them. But if not? We shall indicate later steps which may be taken to discover some possible problems.

Also, we notice in this illustration that John's parents could have become a disrupting influence in the marriage and that they already had become a threat to Adele. So it was necessary that John understand Adele's fears and arrange for his parents to be seen by the counselor.

Other problems were also evident. There was his dependence and her independence. He was spoiled and she very self-reliant. His parents were well-to-do and gave him anything he wanted; whereas she had been on her own since early adolescence. He had lived with his parents, but she with her grandmother or away at school. With such large psychological distances between them, it took some five interviews with each one before they were ready to go on with the final one together. At one point, they were close to deciding against marriage with each other. They were able to discuss this objectively with the counselor and with each other. When we came to the final interview, they were more convinced than ever of their love for each other and that they could make a successful marriage.

With this case as background, let us consider some aspects of the personal interviews.

Purposes of the personal interviews

What are the purposes of the personal interviews? The purposes are (1) to provide a permissive atmosphere in which the interviewee may give expression to his feelings and discuss objectively his problems as he approaches one of the greatest crises in his life; (2) instruction in the nature of Christian marriage. It is important to point out, however, that as in all counseling situations, psychological factors are present: emotional tension, transference, countertransference, acceptance, and role playing. The counselor, therefore, must be particularly careful not to use the other person as a therapist for himself; for in so doing he may, to quote Charles Berg, override "the reality or actual purpose for which the interview was arranged. It often happens that we are in such great need to unburden ourselves of our tensions that, to a greater or lesser degree, the other person is used as a therapist irrespective of his unsuitability for the role." [1] The counselor must always keep in mind that the purpose of the interview is to meet the personality needs of the interviewee. What these basic needs are and how the counselor may meet them will be discussed in the next chapter.

The pastoral relationship deepened by premarital counseling

The personal interviews with the man and the woman can be very rewarding in drawing the individuals close to the minister in a happy pastoral relationship. The chances are that never before have they sat down with a counselor, especially a minister, to discuss themselves: their successes and failures; their inadequacies and capabilities; their likes and dislikes; their ideals of self, home and society, and their hopes, fears and anxieties. If the counselor has a real love for people and a sincere desire to help the couple build a good marriage, it will soon be apparent to the interviewee who will respond eagerly and appreciatively. After all, the counselor is entering upon a crisis with these two people which is any situation (in this case marriage) which arises to cause a change in direction in a person's life.

We meet with many crises daily. Someone has said that man passes through only three major crises: birth, marriage, and death.

---

[1] Charles Berg, *The First Interview with a Psychiatrist* (London: George Allen and Unwin, Ltd., 1955), p. 32.

Birth is not of one's making. Death may be postponed by careful living, but come it will. Marriage, however, is entirely of one's own choosing. It is a crisis that normally does not come upon one suddenly. Most people look forward to marriage and plan for it. Not all are aware of it as a crisis until the marriage vows have been spoken. As I have said, from that time on the two individuals will never again be the same. Their thinking, strivings, plannings will all be interrelated. That is why marriage is such a great and solemn occasion, not only for the two parties who thereby "become one flesh" but also because of the new individuals—new creations —which may come out of the marriage. There may be far reaching consequences, as witness, for example, the marriages out of which have come the great men and women who have contributed to the advancement of the human race. Or again, one might list the marriages out of which have come men and women who have left their mark on civilization in bloodshed and destruction as they schemed to further their own selfish ambitions. Yes, marriage is a serious matter. Only God Himself really knows how serious. Therefore, to have the privilege of giving an individual premarital counseling should stimulate the minister to approach it prayerfully and with much preparation through the study of human behavior, on which any successful counseling depends, and of the institution of marriage itself.

So it is that when the minister sits down with the prospective bride or groom he is at the threshold of a new sort of pastoral relationship. If the minister is able to convey to the interviewee his concern to be of help and if he can create a permissive atmosphere that will give reassurance and inspire confidence, the boundaries of the therapy or counseling will be drawn only by the time and limitations of the counselor and the couple.

Expectations

As in all good counseling, the minister must ask himself, "What does this person expect of me?" For in premarital counseling the person is most likely there because the Church has said that he must receive instruction in the nature of Christian marriage. Before he heard of this canon law he may never have dreamed that he would sit down for a private conference with the minister to discuss some of his most intimate life problems, especially those relating to his marriage. So he may be quite apprehensive.

What then does this person expect? Probably he expects the counselor to tell him about how to make a successful marriage. He may come with the idea, "Here I am, now what do we do?" Or he may be thinking of some problems that have already arisen in the courtship which have produced feelings of anxiety much as Adele had about the happiness of the marriage. He may come hoping that the counselor will give him advice, or reassurance, or even confirm his doubts that the marriage can succeed and so help him to terminate the courtship.

This was the case of a young man who had fallen in love with a girl whose religious background and church were very different from his own and about which they had already engaged in serious arguments. He came for counseling, expecting the counselor to tell him to break off the engagement. This, of course, the counselor refused to do. But after three interviews with him (it was impossible to see the girl because she lived in another city) and after the young man had discussed it further with her, the couple decided it would be best for them not to marry each other.

If the interview is handled skillfully the interviewee's expectations will soon become apparent. But the counselor should keep before him the question: What does this person expect of me?

Flexibility of the interviews

Although these personal interviews are somewhat structured— that is, they may follow more or less a plan as outlined below— they must be flexible enough to go wherever the needs or problems of the interviewee indicate. In fact, because of the time element, it has sometimes been necessary to spend all the counseling periods on certain personality problems which, unless resolved, might have doomed the marriage to failure. Personality problems are those growing out of an overprotected childhood (as in John's case above), lack of authority in the home, sibling rivalry, feeling of rejection as a child resulting from the death of a parent, or death of both parents necessitating being reared by relatives (as in Adele's case), etc. Such problems of personality adjustment may be foremost in the mind of the interviewee which was obviously so of Adele.

In fact, upon understanding the nature of premarital counseling and the intention of the counselor to help one resolve such problems, the real expectations of the interviewee may be chiefly in this direction. Until these personality problems are dealt with, it may be futile to talk about other aspects of building a marriage such as sex, finance, and in-laws. There is little use in talking about finances when the person's identification with his father is so complete in the unsavory aspects of his personality that he may only duplicate the unhappy marriage of his parents.

One woman had so many problems stemming from an unhappy childhood that some ten interviews were required before she seemed ready for the crisis of marriage. She is now very happily married with three fine children and a husband who brags of her role as a wife. Without premarital counseling, it would be hard to see how that marriage could have survived. Every interview thus becomes a vast unexplored land and the counselor should be prepared to go in whatever direction the interviewee leads the way; for he would not be going in that direction if there were not some problem, some fear, some anxiety, propelling him.

Using the background schedule: a case history

The Background Schedule gives a concise and quick reconnaissance of the areas in which problems may occur in the prospective marriage. We shall point this out briefly with the following couple.

Ed and Carrie had been going together a year and a half and

had been engaged three months. They came for their first interview two months before the wedding date. Ed was handsome and tall; Carrie was quite pretty, petite, and vivacious in a shy sort of way.

The Background Schedule showed Ed to be 22 years of age (3) [2] and a junior in college (11). Carrie was 20 years of age (3). She had completed high school (11) and a secretarial course (12).

The following areas stood out as requiring special attention in the counseling sessions:

1. The longest period Ed had spent in one residence before he was 21 years of age had been 3 years (14); whereas, Carrie had spent all her life in one residence (14).

2. Ed's father was a bookkeeper (18); Carrie's father, a business executive (18).

3. Ed's parents were divorced, neither had remarried (25) and both were living (26,27). They were divorced when Ed was 5 years old (28). There had been no signs of affection between them (29). Since they were in conflict all the time (30), Ed appraised their marriage as having been very unhappy (31). Carrie's parents were warmly affectionate and demonstrative (29). They quarrelled, but made up (30). She appraised their marriage as very happy (31).

These areas were taken up in the personal interviews. There were other areas also discussed, but those preceding will be used here by way of illustrating the use of the Background Schedule.

1. Since Ed had moved quite a number of times, it was necessary to determine what effect this had had upon his feeling of security and his reaction to repeatedly making friends and then losing them. Had this made him reluctant to make friends or to be indifferent to people? Ed expressed some feeling of insecurity because of many moves and changing schools. Ventilation helped him considerably as he discussed the reasons for the moves and went over verbally the disappointments involved in breaking friendships.

---

[2] The numbers in parentheses refer to items on the Background Schedule. See Appendix VI.

However, he seemed to be quite well adjusted to other people and had developed an outgoing personality. This was due no doubt to the influence of his mother who had had training as a social worker and made friends easily. Her influence upon him was very strong, but she did not let him become overly dependent upon her. Ed admired his mother and appreciated what she had done in rearing him and his older sister. He got along well with his sister and with other girls (24). He felt comfortable with the opposite sex, which meant that he would be able to promote a good comradeship with Carrie. Also, he and Carrie enjoyed, in general, the same activities (17).

2. Ed was concerned about the difference in the economic background of the two families. His father had contributed nothing to his wife's and children's support; consequently, his mother had had to work. Then, as Ed and his sister grew older, they had had to work too. There were no luxuries, only necessities in their home. On the contrary, Carrie's family was well-to-do. She never lacked for anything she really wanted. Her father had given her a car as a graduation present. Now they were marrying while Ed was still in college. He was on a very good scholarship, however; and Carrie had a good secretarial job.

We discussed the economic difference between the families and possible problems which might arise. They decided that they would live on the scholarship and Carrie's salary until Ed finished college. They would not accept help from her parents. She discussed this problem with her parents who felt also that it would not do for Carrie to have her allowance or receive financial aid from them. Carrie said that she did not expect Ed to keep her "in the style to which she had been accustomed." The important point here is that both faced together, frankly and objectively, the economic difference between their families and arrived at an understanding.

3. The matter of Ed's parents' divorce, his feelings about it, its possible effect upon his marriage, were thoroughly gone into. We shall mention three points especially.

a) After the divorce Ed's father came to see the children occasionally. Sometimes there were violent arguments between his parents. His father met these conflicts by walking out. Ed had begun to do the same thing with Carrie, which made her furious. Sometimes when he was displeased with her, he would "give her the silent treatment"—also one of his father's ways of withdrawing and "punishing." This hurt Carrie very much, and Ed felt guilty. As soon as Ed began to realize that he was following his father's behavior pattern, he began to change at once. He liked Carrie's father. Her father spoke his mind in arguments with his wife and they were soon over the conflict. His wife also spoke her mind. They quarrelled and made up. Ed's parents quarrelled and quit. During the two-months of premarital counseling Ed made remarkable progress in learning to express disagreement and show anger in a mature manner.

Ed expressed some fear that, if things did not go right in his marriage, he might leave as his father had done. He hated divorce and knew the unhappiness which may follow, but at the same time he wondered if he would seek it in some family crisis. Considerable time was spent in helping him make an objective analysis of his parents' home and conditions leading up to the divorce and to discriminate between their home and his home to be. We discussed the roles of husband, wife, father and mother, the rejection of the unwholesome family patterns in his home, and the adoption of wholesome ones he was aware of in Carrie's home, as well as in books and pamphlets dealing with family problems. In other words, he was helped to see that he need not blindly or unconsciously follow his family pattern, but could appropriate other and better patterns.

b) It developed in the interview that one of the causes of divorce in Ed's family was his father's excessive drinking. From Ed's description, it was quite clear that his father was an alcoholic. Ed had begun to drink to excess on several occasions. This led to a discussion of alcoholism, its symptoms, possible causes and treatment. With considerable relief, Ed began to see his father as a sick person in need of treatment, not condemnation. Also, it led to serious thinking on Ed's part regarding his own drinking.

Carrie was very much concerned about Ed's drinking, lest he become like his father. Her parents were total abstainers. She did not want Ed to bring beer or liquor into their home ever. They had already quarrelled at times over his drinking. We, also, had a full discussion of alcoholism with the result that Carrie felt less emotional about it and could discuss it more objectively. Ed and Carrie were able to reevaluate the drinking question as it would relate to the kind of home they wished to build.

c) Another problem growing out of Ed's family background was his failure to show affection for Carrie. This disturbed her because her family was warmly affectionate and demonstrative. Ed wanted to show Carrie affection, but was afraid to lest he lose control and "go all the way." On one occasion this nearly happened. They both had felt shame and guilt. In the personal interviews the problem of demonstrative affection was discussed resulting in a decision on their part to be reserved in their show of affection during their courtship. After the discussion each one expressed relief for having brought up the problem of intimacy in courtship and for help in finding an acceptable way to be affectionate within defined limits. Later in the courtship, Carrie said that Ed was learning to be affectionate and that both felt comfortable, secure and happy in their premarital relationship.

It is hoped that this brief case history has illustrated some of the leads given in the Background Schedule, indicating areas in which may lie serious problems of adjustment.

Getting the interview started

Now there are several ways in which the personal interview may be started. We take our lead from the reconnaissance material provided in the first interview with the couple. What seem to be the psychological problems which may affect the marital adjustment? What of the psychological distances between the couple?

By psychological distance we mean differences in general cultural factors such as race, education, religion, and economic background.

Having determined from the "Background Schedule" and the first interview with the couple where problems would most likely occur, we may ask the individual such questions as: "How do you feel about the difference in education between you and your fiance?" "or difference in religion?" Having explained the meaning of psychological distance between persons, another way to begin would be to ask, "What psychological distances do you feel exist between you and your fiance?"

I sometimes also ask the individual, "How do you feel about your fiance? Do you notice anything in his personality or character, mannerisms, or family traditions that you think may some day become a problem between you?" After a moment of thought, the interviewee may name something as, for example: "He is jealous" "He is overpossessive" or "We quarrel a lot." Ample opportunity must be given for full expression of what is meant. Again, the interviewee may say "Oh, he's perfect. I can't think of anything that could ever be a problem between us." My reply is usually, "Well, that is wonderful. If there are no problems to talk about regarding him, then let's talk about you. What kind of person are you?" This invariably brings a smile, thoughtfulness and then generally a really honest attempt at self-appraisal. Often, as this proceeds, the interpersonal relationship with the fiance begins to be revealed and some criticism of him (or her) comes out. The way is cleared then for much frank discussion, leading to ventilation, reduction of hostility, insight, and objective thinking.

Mary came from a family of college graduates. She herself was a junior in college. John had only a high school education. How did Mary feel about this? She did not like it and had already begun to "work on him" by prodding him; in fact she said, "I know I nag him about going to college. But I am afraid he cannot succeed with only a high school diploma." Already nagging before the vows were said! What would it be afterwards? John expressed resentment over her superiority. "If she will leave me alone I will go to college. I know that she is right." This problem appeared so paramount, and their reactions so spontaneous that this seemed to be the place to start the interview.

Some counselors will take issue with this questioning method of starting the personal interview, but it must be kept in mind—and I reiterate—that premarital counseling in the Church is different from other counseling in that individuals usually come not on their own initiative, but at the request or even insistence of the minister. Also, premarital counseling involves instruction in those factors which constitute a good marriage, such as mutual understanding, handling finances, getting along with in-laws and establishing a wholesome religious basis. Both instruction and counseling are integral to premarital counseling. The minister-counselor should prepare himself to give sound instruction as well as to do skilled counseling. Not only must he give information, but also, he must correct misinformation.

Further suggestions toward objective thinking

In helping the interviewee look at himself objectively, I have found it helpful to ask questions regarding:

Maturity. How do you evaluate yourself as an emotionally mature person? This is a good question for getting into the meaning of maturity, and for discussing successful marriage as a union between mature persons. Do you cooperate readily with others in achieving a common goal? Do you give and take in planning? Are you an individualist? The lone wolf type? Are you teachable? Willing to learn from others? How well do you communicate with others?

Frustration. How do you react to frustration? Do you give up, cry, sulk, withdraw, strike out at or blame others for your failure to foresee a situation and plan against failure? Are you able to take an objective view of a bad situation and plan calmly what to do?

Tolerance. Do you appreciate opinions different from your own?

Are you a "know-it-all"? Do you welcome ideas and suggestions from others and integrate them into your own thinking and planning? Are you able to share your thoughts and feelings with others, even though they may criticize them? Can you see your own faults? What are some of your faults which may block good interpersonal relationships?

Understanding. Do you understand people, especially the significant persons in your environment? Do you understand your fiance, for example? Are you a good listener? Or are you so concerned about yourself that you are unable to enter into the problems of others?

Love. What are the components of love? How would you define Christian love? What are its elements i.e., self-sacrifice; God's love; a relationship like that between Christ and the Church; consideration for the feelings, desires, and sensibilities of the other person; kindness; gentleness; tenderness; responsiveness; empathy? Mature love responds to the needs of the other person.

In discussing love one might consider:

Eros: physical or sexual love. Some couples never get beyond this stage and may marry only to satisfy sexual needs. A marriage formed on this basis has little chance of succeeding.

Philia. "The Father loves (philia) the Son, and shows him all that he himself is doing."[3] This higher level of love is expressed in companionship and mutual sharing: the exquisite joy of merely being in the presence of the loved one and discussing future plans.

Agape: benevolence. This is love that calls forth sacrifice for the object of one's love. "Greater love (agape) has no man than this, that a man lay down his life for his friends."[4] This love is outgoing in the service of others. It is deep and broad enough to allow for the proper loves and interests of the loved one. It embraces the whole family and reaches out into the community in service.

A true marriage develops along all three kinds of love. Any one

[3] John 5:20.
[4] John 15:13.

kind is insufficient. Couples should be helped in analyzing along what lines their love is developing.

The questions above are merely suggestions for stimulating the individual to think objectively about himself, his fiance, and his environment.[5] The counselor should be warned that if he gives the answers, the purpose will be defeated. He is there only to encourage the person to talk out therapeutically his ideas and feelings in his presence and find his own answers. The pastor, no doubt, could deliver a good sermon answering every question beautifully and convincingly to himself, especially since he has a captive audience. The skilled counselor, however, will bear patiently with the individual as he tries to put into words his thinking, perhaps for the first time, on these personality problems.

Roles

It is rather trite to quote Shakespeare, "All the world's a stage," but one does find oneself cast in not one, but many roles as one takes part in the drama of human living: the role of son, father, husband, brother, employee, employer, lawyer, doctor, minister. Both sexes have various roles to play. Some adjust quite readily in passing from one role to another while others find it very difficult.

A man who had been a bachelor until past thirty, became engaged, and after some months married. During the courtship, all went smoothly and they had wonderful times together. He had gone with many girls and was duplicating what had taken place with others. He was skilled in playing the role of man-about-town, kept his own hours, ate when and where he pleased, had a good salary and was answerable to no one but himself. During this period, even after asking the woman to marry him, he never gave any thought to the problem he was soon to face— that of assuming a new role, the role of husband. After the marriage he was no longer the considerate lover; he showed no patience

[5] All of these are leading questions which imply the "right" answer and are intended to focus the individual upon positive rather than negative attitudes.

and no affection. This man had to learn how to be a husband and what was required in the role. The only pattern he had to go by was that of his father, which was not a good one. An actor, by copying a good actor may learn much, but can ruin his career under the influence of a poor one. So, playing the roles open to one, one unconsciously follows one's parents or other significant figures. The trouble is, however, one follows indiscriminately the good and the bad patterns of behavior they set. As a person matures, one should try to be objective enough to reject these bad traits, while building the good traits into one's personality structure and behavior patterns.

The concept of an individual's role is very important in the marriage relationship. The two great differences, of course, are between male and female. These two are not naturally in competition. There are roles suited to each, and when assumed cooperation becomes characteristic of the sexes. Men do not want wives who compete for dominance. The male is by nature aggressive. He is the protector of the family and physically the strongest member. The wife is non-aggressive and wants to feel protected. The wife who tries to "wear the pants" may enter into such competition with her husband as to make adjustment in all areas very difficult. Of course, we do find retiring, passive men who marry aggressive women. When this abnormal situation is recognized by both parties, a happy adjustment can be made. Sex dissimilarities present a complicated picture. To quote Landis:

Some of the restrictions placed on women by our moral and economic double standard have no justification; they are simply relics from less enlightened times. Others have a logical and firm basis in the scheme of things as set up by nature, and legislating against them or agitating about them will not alter the facts. The facts concerning the nature, physical make-up, and functioning of men and of women point neither to equality nor to inequality. The more accurate concept is that major dissimilarities do exist, but the words "equal" and "unequal" are inapplicable when we compare the capacities and abilities of the sexes.

Men and women are complementary to each other; an acceptance of their biological and cultural differences is important if they are to fulfill their roles constructively and happily.[6]

Roles are changing and mixed. In the past, the role of husband and wife in the home was more fixed than today. It is changing rapidly. Many husbands do chores which in the past only wives did, such as those connected with housekeeping and the care of the children. In many households husbands don aprons and wash dishes, sweep, make beds, bathe the children and even cook. Many wives work or are busy with church and school activities which take them out of the home a considerable part of the time. It is not uncommon to find wives managing the family finances: doing the banking, writing the checks, and giving the husband an allowance.

Thus, not only do we play many roles, but the roles are changing and mixed.

In premarital counseling it is most important that the counselor help the couple to face realistically the roles they will find themselves in after marriage. It will make adjustments easier and will prevent each from expecting the other to assume roles for which he is incapable.

The minister-counselor's role. It is also essential that the minister-counselor recognize his role in the counseling process. Being a minister, he is expected to uphold the Christian ideal and standards of marriage. If he has been in his parish several years, he may have known one or both individuals from their childhood. They may hold him in an affectionate relationship similar to that in which they look upon their parents. Thus, he may be a real father figure who will speak to them with that authority. Certainly, he will have built up a feeling of trustworthiness and respect for his role as a "father" within the church family of his own parish. These interviews can be a source of inspiration for the minister if he understands his role and accepts its responsibilities.

[6] Landis and Landis, *Building a Successful Marriage,* pp. 22-23.

Deep therapy not to be attempted

Deep therapy should not be attempted unless one is qualified to do it. If serious personality problems appear,[7] the person should be referred to a mental health clinic, a psychiatrist, or a psychologist trained in counseling. Of course, every minister has to talk with people who are neurotic or psychotic to a varying degree. He may be the first to detect personality deviations and to recommend treatment to the family. But it is not always easy to get treatment for these people, and, there being no other alternative, the minister may have to listen to them many times. To reject them might add to their deterioration. My experience has been that most people are greatly helped by catharsis or ventilation: just the talking out of their problems in the presence of the counselor in whom they have confidence. Every good counselor has patiently listened for an hour or more with scarcely a word said by him, and has had the person, at the end of the interview say, "Thank you. You have helped me so much. I feel better now." It must be emphasized that the minister-counselor should not attempt therapy with seriously disturbed persons. They should be referred to the professionally qualified for treatment.

The time element

The time element is also an important factor in premarital counseling. A great deal of material must be covered in a limited number of interviews. Obviously, everything cannot be dealt with. The counselor must select problems which he feels are basic ones as revealed in the interviews, according to the concern of the individuals. The same kind of selection must be done in matters calling for instruction. It is impossible in eight, ten or even twenty interviews to cover everything. And many couples

[7] This refers to sexual deviations, homicidal and/or suicidal fears, sadism, masochism, psychotic behavior, and the like.

would not continue to come, or even begin, if they thought the counseling would go beyond eight or ten interviews.

This means that premarital counseling has to be structured and fitted into time limitations. It is a mixture of directive and non-directive. It must be flexible. It is my experience that this method works in that a good majority of the couples who have been through it report happy marriages.

Summary

The author has attempted to indicate the nature of the counseling method as related to premarital counseling and the various directions it may take in the personal interviews. These must be flexible so that the expectations and needs of the individual may be considered by the counselor and met by instruction and counseling within the time limit available.

Several suggestions were made for getting the interview started. The information given in the reconnaissance material is of great value in this regard.

The counselor must be prepared not only to give information, but, also, to correct misinformation. By questions and discussion he helps the interviewee to look at himself objectively, resulting in an acceptance of the new roles he must assume in marriage.

5

The second interview with the couple

This interview normally takes place a few days before the wedding. It summarizes all the other interviews, and introduces the couple to the spiritual aspect of their marriage, based on a study of the marriage service.[1]

It is important to impress upon the couple that they are to be users of the information and insights gained in the personal interviews. If these interviews were spread out over a period of several months, the couple would have already done a great deal of reality-testing thereby making adjustments in their relationships. Also,

[1] The Form of Solemnization of Matrimony in the Book of Common Prayer. Ministers will naturally use the marriage service of their own denominations for this interview. The Episcopal service is used in this chapter by way of illustration and because it contains the basic ideas found in other marriage services.

it should be made clear to them that religion has much to offer in reinforcing the adjustments made and deepening the insights gained. Religion adds eternal value to these things.

The interview may conclude with the signing of the Declaration of Intention, if not signed previously (see Chapter 3), the License, the Parish Register and the Marriage Service Booklet. Of course, the minister would not sign any of the documents until after the wedding ceremony. Some ministers prefer to have these documents signed either just before or just after the ceremony. Witnesses must sign after the ceremony. Even if the bride and groom sign the documents after the wedding, it is good to have these at hand for this interview, so that they may be explained. In addition to these documents, there should be on hand a Bible, a *Book of Common Prayer*, *In Holy Matrimony*, or a similar book and a booklet of daily devotions suitable for family prayer.

By the time this interview is held, a good friendly relationship should have developed between the couple and the minister. Also, the couple should have come to know each other better. They will have explored many of their personality problems with each other in the light of the personal interviews. This is one reason why the premarital counseling should be stretched over a period of about three months. Sometimes it has to be compressed within two or three weeks.

Once, after having to do this because a couple had to meet some time schedule, I asked another couple who were nearing the completion of their counseling schedule, which had extended over some four months, that, if they had it to do over, would they prefer having it telescoped into two or three weeks. They emphatically said no, explaining that they felt the premarital counseling had definitely enriched their courtship, by enabling them to see each other more objectively and to work through some of their personality problems. Of course, the minister and the couple feel close, having faced together and talked over some of the basic personality problems of the couple and their relationship to each other. So this second interview with the couple should be less strained than the first, and more congenial to a discussion of the spiritual side of the marriage than may have been the case had this been made the subject of the first interview.

The expectations of the couple

The pastor must ask himself, "What do these two people expect of me in this last interview?" The beginning of their life together is now imminent. The threshold will soon be crossed. The personal interviews, the books they had read have all pointed toward this crisis: the beginning of their married life. Since they have come to the Church for their marriage, they probably have some deep religious convictions about the sanctity of marriage. So, they probably expect the minister-counselor to reassure them that this marriage will be strengthened by God and through the Holy Spirit at work in their lives. They may expect him to relate their marriage to a strong religious foundation on which they can build securely a life-long union.

The purpose of the interview

So the purpose of this interview is to do just that: To point out the spiritual values involved in a Christian marriage and how those values may be realized.

The Church's interest in their marriage

Another purpose of this interview is to enable them to understand further the Church's interest in their marriage. No one is more interested in their marriage than the Church acting through the minister. All through the interviews it is hoped that they will have reached this conclusion. If they have, or if they do before the interviews are over, then they will know that, if problems arise which they cannot resolve, they can go to the minister or to a marriage-counselor who will help them.

Church canons

One problem the Church has with couples who have made unsatisfactory adjustments in marriage and are contemplating separation or divorce is to get them to seek counsel from a minister first.   Canon 16 reads:

Where marital unity is imperilled by dissension, it shall be the duty of either or both parties, before contemplating legal action, to lay the matter before a Minister of this Church; and it shall be the duty of such Minister to labor that the parties be reconciled.   [See Appendix I.]

The minister should be familiar enough with psychology and marital problems to know whether or not he should enter into a marriage counseling program with the couple or refer them to someone else: a minister trained in counseling, a psychiatrist, a psychologist trained in this field, or a professional marriage counselor.   The American Association of Marriage Counselors, Inc., is a reliable organization composed of counselors with the proper training.   The Institute of Family Relations and the Family Service Association can also recommend reliable counselors. Couples should be warned against consulting counselors who are not listed with a reliable organization.

The marriage service

It would be presumptuous for me to tell the minister how to deal with the marriage service. He has doubtless explained it and preached on it often. I shall mention only a few points which I have found are helpful in premarital counseling.

Marriage, a partnership: God, Church, State and the couple

My plan is to point out in the Exhortation and Charge to the congregation[2] that marriage concerns more people than just the couple. Marriage is a partnership, but not only between the husband and wife. This partnership includes first of all, God, who according to Hebrew-Christian tradition and teaching, instituted marriage for the safeguard of the family and society. God is, therefore, vitally concerned with the marriage and will do all in His power to strengthen it and help the couple make it a happy and successful one. A marriage that develops out of sincere love and the intention of the parties to build a godly home, has God's blessing.

Because we believe marriage to be instituted of God, signifying unto us the mystical union between Christ and His Church, we surround it with all the solemnity and reverence of which we are capable, lifting it to as high a spiritual plane as possible. To further spiritualize Holy Matrimony, the *Book of Common Prayer* provides a Collect, Epistle, and Gospel to be used at a marriage communion service.[3] There is nothing more meaningful than to have the Holy Communion either on the morning of the wedding or at the time of the wedding. Thus the Church makes every effort to impress upon her people the sacredness of Holy Matrimony.

The congregation present represents two important institutions: Church and State. Now both of these institutions are partners in the marriage. Both have required the couple to sign certain agreements: the Church, the Declaration of Intention; individual states, the Marriage License. Here we think it is well to have the couple read over again the Declaration of Intention and to review

[2] *Book of Common Prayer,* The Form of Solemnization of Holy Matrimony, p. 300.

[3] *Ibid.,* p. 267.

some of the points raised in the personal interviews—however, the counselor must be very careful not to betray any confidences told him in the personal interviews. The Declaration of Intention is the Church's partnership agreement with the couple. The Church on its part will provide special assistance to the couple in making theirs a permanent and happy union. These assistances include, of course, the Holy Communion and other services of the Church, Holy Baptism for the children, and later confirmation, religious education, and family prayer. In all these ways God mediates Himself to the couple, their children, their home. Beginning their marriage at the altar, they should be encouraged to keep their marriage close to the altar by participating together in the whole life of the Church. Here is another opportunity to impress upon them the importance of being in the same church.

The congregation, being also citizens of the State, represents states which require that the couple sign the license, a legal document. Thus the state joins the partnership by providing a legal status to the marriage. By law neither spouse can willy-nilly step out of it. If they wish to dissolve the marriage they must follow the due process of the state's laws and the Church's canons.

Thus Church and State recognize marriage as a part of their structure and any threat to a marriage is a threat to Church and State, for the home is the primary and basic institution of society. Every divorce weakens the State, and every divorce of a Church couple weakens the Church; society itself is weakened at its base.

Every Christian marriage is a partnership consisting of God, the Church, the State and the couple, and later (perhaps) of children. All of this makes of marriage a most solemn and sacred event.

Marriage, a mystical union

We have found it particularly effective to read with the couple the reference to "the mystical union that is betwixt Christ and his Church" in the Letter to the Ephesians:

Wives, be subject to your husbands, as to the Lord. For the husband is the head of the wife as Christ is the head of the church, his body, and is himself its Savior. As the church is subject to Christ, so let wives also be subject in everything to their husbands. Husbands, love your wives, as Christ loves the church and gave himself up for her, that he might sanctify her, having cleansed her by the washing of water with the word, that the church might be presented before him in splendor, without spot or wrinkle or any such thing, that she might be holy and without blemish. Even so husbands should love their wives as their own bodies. He who loves his wife loves himself. For no man ever hates his own flesh, but nourishes and cherishes it, as Christ does the church, because we are members of his body. "For this reason a man shall leave his father and mother and be joined to his wife, and the two shall become one." This is a great mystery, and I take it to mean Christ and the church; however, let each one of you love his wife as himself, and let the wife see that she respects her husband.[4]

I shall not go into a full exposition of this reference. But I would like specially to point out the practical value of the wife's being subject to her husband.

In our modern society we find the application of this in the wife's acceptance of her husband as the breadwinner and of his employment or profession as sometimes the controlling factor as to where and how they are to live. The wife does have to submit to her husband's work. If he is a doctor, she must realize that he will keep inconvenient hours and be at the call of his patients. If he is a traveling man, she must submit to lonely days and nights. These points should have been raised in the personal interviews, but need to be indicated again in the presence of both parties.

Mark had received a fine promotion in his company, but it required him to move to another city in another state. His wife refused to go (refused to be subject to him) and insisted that he give up the promotion, of which he had dreamed and for which he had worked for several years. She even suggested he go into some other business so that she might remain where they were.

[4] Ephesians 5:22-33.

He felt he could do neither. After several interviews, the wife came to realize what she was asking and what her duty to her husband required of her. She agreed to go. A year or two later she expressed her happiness over her decision. At first thought "let wives also be subject in everything to their husbands" sounds a bit out of tune with modern ideas of woman's independence, but actually in a marriage, where the responsibility for the material prosperity of the family depends so largely upon the husband, there are many instances when the wife must be subject to him.

The home, a unity

The Christian home is one in which husband and wife seek to perfect such a unity that all members of the family will find love and security.

Agnes was in great distress because the family seemed to be "breaking apart." Since she and her husband seldom agreed about disciplining the children and were divided on so many issues, there was no unity to which anyone in the family could look for authority. "Everyone was a law unto himself." Each one seemed to use the home as a means of satisfying his personal pleasure. No one wanted to give anything in return. This home was in the process of disintegrating.

A *cell of the Kingdom of God.* When a Christian man and a Christian woman are united in Holy Matrimony, we have a cell of the Kingdom of God. Here we have the elements for the perfect and complete expression of love. In fact, it is doubtful if outside the marriage state one can know the full depth and meaning of love. For, between husband and wife there is possible a more complete sharing and self-denial than is found in any other social unit. When children come into this cell, not only is it widened, but the channels through which love may be expressed are infinitely increased. There we see the self-sacrificing love of Christ set before us over and over again: father and mother unhesitatingly, voluntarily, giving themselves for the well-being and happiness of each other and of the children.   The principles underlying the Christian family rest upon the premise of the reality of God.   And so in the home, no less than in any social group, when the members live in harmony with God and His divine plan, peace, justice and happiness prevail, and for them, "The Kingdom of God is achieved." For the Kingdom of God is essentially a relationship between persons.

The husband's responsibility

In any normal marriage in our culture the husband is responsible for providing the family with food, clothes and shelter.   It is his God-given privilege in the nature of things.   Therefore, his profession or career and his happiness and peace of mind are all essential to his fulfilling his responsibility.   Sometimes, momentous decisions have to be made.   After consultation with his wife, it may be that he must do the deciding.   For he can best care for the family when he is in the kind of work he likes and is best qualified to do.   The wife then must accept her husband's decision and encourage him in it.   A disgruntled, half-hearted wife is a great handicap to her husband and can easily ruin his career and the marriage.

Am I speaking too boldly for the husband? Let us see what St. Paul says his treatment of his wife should be:

Husbands, love your wives, as Christ loved the Church and gave Himself up for her, that she might be holy and without blemish . . . Even so husbands should love their wives as their own bodies.[5]

Christ so loved the Church that He gave His life for it.   So should a husband cherish and protect and revere his wife.   There is really no difference in their attitude toward each other, if they are Christians.   For each will love the other as his own body; and each will strive in every way to please the other and to make the home a happy and wholesome place.

[5] Ibid., vss. 22, 28.

Love, the foundation

There is only one foundation on which to build a Christian home, and that is love. This love is the same love as that between Christ and the Church. In a sense, only real Christians believe they can build such a home, because only they realize what Christ did for the Church and for them, and knowing the extent of Christ's love they are compelled to show for each other, as far as in them lies, the same love with all its unselfishness, forgivingness, and constancy.

Thus, we see then, that as Christians it is only in and through the Church that the real unity in the home is to be attained. For if husband and wife and children are members of the Church, then Christ should be the center of the home and all so intent upon serving Him that they will find themselves serving each other in His name and for His sake. Their mutual love for Christ will spiritualize and deepen their love for each other.

Without spot or wrinkle

The whole passage in Ephesians is rich with sound instruction which every minister will exploit to the fullest. There is one other point I wish to make here. "Husbands, love your wives, as Christ loved the church and gave himself up for her . . . that the church might be presented before Him in splendor, without spot or wrinkle or any such thing . . ." We often ask the groom to project himself and his bride thirty years into the future and imagine his wife presented before him. What will she be like? Will her face be drawn and marked with lines of anxiety, fear and insecurity? Or will it be marked with the natural wrinkles of aging, wrinkles or lines that reveal character, sacrifice, beauty of soul, peace and security? It is largely up to him to determine how she will look. And likewise it is largely up to her to determine how he will look.

After the passage has been fully discussed, in reference to their marriage and life together, we go on through the rest of the Exhortation and Charge.

Betrothal vows

Let us take up next the betrothal vows. These require first of all that the couple live together after God's ordinance. This does not concern civil ordinance. The Christian's duty to what is right is never limited to a civil ordinance, which is man-made, but to God's ordinance. Therefore, because the civil law makes divorce possible, it is worthwhile to remind the couple that the civil ordinance is not to be used as an excuse to enter Christian marriage with the thought "Well, if it doesn't succeed, I can get a divorce." The marriage service requires that couples live together after God's ordinance—following all the laws of God, living together in righteousness and true holiness.

Further, the betrothal pledge, as well as the marriage vow, binds the two parties to each other "for better for worse, for richer or poorer, in sickness and in health, to love and to cherish till death us do part." [6] The marriage service makes no provision for the dissolution of the marriage bonds except by death.

One cannot know the vicissitudes and changes that will come in life. Disease and accidents come, unfortunate habits develop; but where a true Christian marriage has been consummated between two Christian people, who love each other and above all love God, grace can be found to overcome all difficulties, especially if they will avail themselves of good marriage counseling from their minister. For two earnest Christian people, who sincerely love God and His Church, and strive to do His will, receive the grace and strength to suffer and persevere under heartbreaking handicaps. We have known of such cases and found their home sanctified with the Presence of Christ Himself.

[6] *Book of Common Prayer,* p. 301.

The Lambeth Conference of 1948 recognized that:

There are men and women who, in spite of much unhappiness, are nobly struggling to carry out their marriage vows in sad and heartbreaking conditions—conditions which might drive many to seek relief in divorce. It is the duty of the Church to give them all the sympathy and encouragement and help that is possible, and to guard against the occurrence of such tragic situations by a strengthening of the ideals of marriage through instruction and preparation, and by pastoral care. Discipline will not be resented if those who break the Church's law understand what the law is and that the aim of discipline is to rebuild, not to punish.[7]

This statement was reaffirmed by the Lambeth Conference of 1958.

This is a good place to get the couple to think together about the meaning of "Forsaking all others, keep thee only unto her (him) so long as ye both shall live." This forsaking all others seems to apply mainly to in-laws. The couple probably have by now discussed their attitude toward their in-laws who may seek to interfere with the marriage, or who may have to live with them. The principle mentioned in the personal interviews, "my home must come first," should be re-emphasized so that each may understand the other's position in reference to any particular in-law. And also if any difficulty should arise, each should understand that it is the responsibility of the one whose parents or relatives are involved, as in-laws of the other, to take the initiative in resolving the problem. Other points in the Betrothal will of course be discussed.

The marriage vows

Two phrases in the marriage vows which always require explaining are "Thereto I plight thee my troth" and "thereto I give thee

---

[7] *The Lambeth Conference 1948*, (London: The Society for the Promoting of Christian Knowledge, 1948, Part II), p. 97.

my troth." Very few couples know the meaning of the words "plight" and "troth." Plight means to pledge, or to swear; and troth means fidelity, or faithfulness. Faithfulness in all things: love, work, home-building, role as husband and wife, use of money, and faithfulness in one's sex life. There is so much sexual promiscuity today that I feel faithfulness to each other in their sex life should be stated frankly and plainly in the presence of both.

The prayers

The prayers[8] offer many suggestions for helping the couple discover their duty toward each other in building a Christian home and a successful marriage. Again, I shall not take these up in detail, but mention only some of the chief ideas.

Note how faithfulness is introduced in support of the marriage vows: "that they, living faithfully together, may surely perform and keep the vow and covenant betwixt them made"; and this carries over as the basis for remaining in "perfect love and peace together, and live according to thy laws." This is again emphasized in the fourth prayer: "so live together in faithfulness . . . that their home may be a haven of blessing and of peace." I shall not labor the point that there are many ways in which faithfulness is basic to marriage or any covenant. Each minister will develop his own ideas about it and help the couple to find for themselves the implications of it, as it must permeate the whole marriage. The same procedure should be followed with other key words: covenant, love, honor, and cherish. A word about honor, because honoring another surely means courtesy and respect toward another. So many couples drop the courtesies toward each other shown before marriage. Some degenerate into actual rudeness. Courtesy is very important in interpersonal relationships. Other key words that may be explored are patience, wisdom, godliness.

[8] *Book of Common Prayer*, p. 303.

The home, a haven

There is one phrase that seems to sum up all that has been said throughout the interviews and which points to the goal of a happy and successful marriage: "that their home may be a haven of blessing and of peace." I have been surprised at the proportionately few people who know the meaning of "haven." Young couples are unacquainted with it, or have only some vague idea about it. It is a beautiful word and very applicable to a good home. Every minister has called at homes in the late afternoon when he might expect to find the husband returning from work, and finds a wife unkempt and unattractive. We have sometimes wondered why a husband who has been working beside a neatly dressed, attractive woman all day would want to come home to a wife who is careless of her appearance. She would never have let him see her like that before marriage. Even though a wife may have had a hard day with the children and housework, she should take a few minutes to freshen up before her husband comes home. Whether she likes it or not, she is still to some extent competing with other women for his attention. Much can be said of the husband, too, who comes home and reduces his clothing to a minimum without regard to his wife's sensibilities. These "little things" can be just the one thing that tips the scale toward home being an agreeable or disagreeable place.

When a man leaves home in the morning and goes through all the conflicts, discouragements, disappointments, sometimes failures of the day in whatever field his work may be, he should be able to carry in his mind a picture of his haven to which he may return at the end of day and find there happiness and peace with a wife who understands and is capable of giving him love and self-confidence. Home should be the place where he can relax and know he is accepted in spite of his weakness and failures. All of this must be said for the wife, too. She may have had a hard day, either at home, or at her outside job. When her husband returns she should be able to find in him love, understanding, and reassurance. So together they must work to make their home this sort of haven. Just signing a marriage license will not produce it, any more than signing a contract will build a house. The two people must work at it and work hard, day in and day out, year by year, "so long as ye both shall live."

The secret of a happy marriage lies not only along the lines of satisfactory adjustments in the areas we have discussed, but also in its spiritual foundation. A home strengthened by the teaching and use of the *Book of Common Prayer* (or other devotional books), enriched with its ancient wisdom, inspired by its prayers and centered in God, will enable husband and wife to establish a haven of happiness and of peace, in which they "may so live together in this life, that in the world to come they may have life everlasting."

Available assistances to a successful marriage

In our Christian concept of marriage a couple does not work alone: God is with them, and the Christian fellowship supports them. Many assistances are available to them—the family altar, regular church participation, and especially frequent reception of the Holy Communion where, kneeling side by side at the place where their marriage vows were first said, they may renew them and ask God's help in building their marriage. Family prayer should be started the first night or first day of marriage. Couples will need some practical suggestions for doing this. Here is a good time to ask if they have a *Book of Common Prayer*.[9] I generally suggest breakfast as perhaps the most convenient time for family prayer—mainly because that has been the custom in my own home. Of course, every couple must work out the time for themselves.

[9] We keep on hand copies of the inexpensive 5 x 7 1/2 cloth *Book of Common Prayer*, which we may sell or give to the couple along with "Forward," the Episcopal booklet of daily devotionals, and suggestions on how to use them.

Signing the documents

After the proclamation of the marriage and the blessing have been discussed the couple may sign the license, marriage booklet, and Parish Register. A short prayer with the couple closes what should have been a wholesome, beneficial experience for the couple and the minister.

The rehearsal

After the rehearsal has been concluded, I have found that the minister has an excellent opportunity to explain briefly to the wedding party the Church's attitude toward marriage and the importance of premarital counseling in preparation for marriage. The Declaration of Intention may be read to further emphasize the importance the Church places upon marriage. Also, it is a good opportunity to point out that marriage is both a happy and a solemn occasion; that the marriage service is a religious one and those attending should prepare themselves for it through prayer and anticipation of receiving a spiritual blessing. Since it is a religious service, all should come to it as they would come to any other religious service, unfortified by anything stronger than coffee. The talk is closed with a prayer and a request to those present to leave the church quietly. Invariably after this, individuals either in the church or at the rehearsal party have expressed their appreciation for what has been said and often have added, "I wish other ministers would do this."

Summary

I have tried to emphasize the spiritual aspects of marriage without encroaching upon the minister-counselor's own interpretations, realizing that every minister has his own concepts of the spiritual nature of marriage. Only a few of the high points have been indicated.

The couple should realize the Church is interested in their marriage and that they can always turn to the Church for help in time of marital difficulty, especially before contemplating legal action.[10]

The marriage service summarizes in the language of religion what has been said to the couple in the language of psychology. Each points toward the goal of wholesome interpersonal relationships resulting in a happy home.

[10] *Constitution and Canons for the Government of the Protestant Episcopal Church in the United States of America*, 1955, p. 44.

6

Counseling couples marrying
under special circumstances

This chapter deals with cases in which pre-marital counseling is indicated because of special problems involving the physically handicapped, couples forced into marriage, widows and widowers, and divorced persons. It is obvious that people involved in these marriages have suffered traumatically because of some misfortune: accident of birth, carelessness, or death of a loved one. How they have adjusted to their particular situations has a direct bearing upon whatever marital adjustment they will make, whether it be their first, second, or third, marriage.

The physically handicapped

Robert Burton (1577-1640) in his *Anatomy of Melancholy* made this poignant observation: "Deformities and imperfections of our bodies, as lameness, crookedness, deafness, be they innate or accidental, torture many men." Coleman comments, "Congenital and acquired defects place the individual under stress and may markedly increase the difficulties of his marital, occupational, and social adjustments. When we realize that there are some 25 million persons in the United States with a chronic disease or permanent physical impairment and that more than half of those under 45 years of age and approximately 16 per cent under 25 years, we begin to grasp the tremendous scope of this problem." [1]

These handicapped individuals are in special need of premarital counseling for the way in which they have learned to evaluate and adjust to their life situation will carry over and may be intensified in marriage. Emotional maladjustment is not caused by the physical handicap itself, but by the attitudes and comments of others and the self-evaluation of the individual. Handicapped people are usually self-conscious and sensitive.

Feelings of inferiority, self-pity, reclusiveness, fear, aggressiveness, hostility, and over-compensation are some of the less desirable reactions that such handicaps may induce. Of course, parental attitudes toward the impairment are crucially important here. Too often, parents of handicapped children develop attitudes of extreme overprotection or rejection or press for accomplishments beyond the child's abilities. In such cases the child is unnecessarily handicapped psychologically in meeting life's problems. [2]

In general, personality maladjustment is more common among physically disabled persons than among physically normal persons although there is clearly no direct causal connection between the handicap and the maladjustment. It is the individual's attitude and evaluation that determine his adjustive reactions.

This means then that premarital counseling offers an opportunity to the physically handicapped individual to discuss his handicap,

[1] James C. Coleman, *Abnormal Psychology and Modern Life* (© 1950 by Scott, Foresman and Company, Chicago), p. 108.
[2] *Ibid.*

how he feels about it, and how the other partner feels about it. We might include here operations which may have left ugly scars hidden by clothing, internal operations such as removal of the uterus and/or ovaries, or sterility, if known. Hidden handicaps can be a great shock to the other partner and become a serious threat to the marriage itself.

Agnes, a very lovely girl, came to make arrangements for premarital counseling. One of the first things she said was, "Jim has a withered foot which is very conspicuous though he walks fairly well. Some of my friends think I should not marry him. But I love him and want to be his wife. His handicap does not seem to bother him." She talked freely about it. They had been to the beach where she had become accustomed to his lameness and there they had talked about it together and he did "funny little things with his toes and laughed."

When Jim came, one of the first things he did was to show his foot. He had been born handicapped and the foot had not developed. He spoke of childhood experiences, feelings of inferiority because he could not engage in games as did other boys, how he learned to compensate by developing his arms and shoulders. He had been anxious about how Agnes would feel toward his handicap but she had reassured him that she was not marrying his "foot" but "himself," for otherwise he was a strong man with handsome features.

After several interviews the handicap seemed of no importance to them, although when they first came it had been uppermost in their minds. They expressed appreciation for having had the opportunity to talk it over with someone "neutral," who was outside the emotional atmosphere of the family constellation.

Things do not always go so smoothly. Attending her first premarital counseling session, a woman who was handicapped by a withered arm complained that in times of family stress and quarreling her husband would make sarcastic remarks about her arm. Consequently, she had become more and more sensitive about it. She finally persuaded her husband to come for counseling. He was reluctant at first to talk about his wife's arm for fear the counselor would tell her. But once he started talking he expressed himself freely. At first he had not wanted to marry her because of it. There had been no one to discuss the matter with. However, he did marry her because he loved her. After marriage he felt embarrassed if she wore an evening dress with no sleeves. As he talked he began to express himself about her personality and her facial beauty. Gradually he began to realize that her withered arm was really very unimportant, and that he could accept it and help her to accept it. Although this was not their only problem, it was more important in the marital relationship than either had realized.

There are cases on record of women who have nursed and married soldiers who were maimed, and other cases of men and women marrying someone who had an affliction resulting from polio, or from an accident. Where there is genuine love and devotion and a good objective understanding of the disability, happy, successful marriages result. Statistics would be hard to find in these cases where a divorce was due mainly to the disability because very few individuals would run the risk of public condemnation which would surely follow the rejection of a partner because of such affliction.

Couples forced into marriage

There are no statistics on the number of couples who are forced into marriage because of pregnancy. Sex relations before marriage are very common. Kinsey's study revealed that of the women interviewed about 50 per cent reported premarital coitus. He also found that for those marrying for the first time at ages 16-20, 47 per cent had premarital coitus by age 20; those marrying at 21-25, 26 per cent, and 26-30, 14 per cent.[3] For males, Kinsey re-

[3] Alfred C. Kinsey, Wardell B. Pomeroy, Clyde E. Martin, and Paul H. Gebhard, *Sexual Behavior in the Human Female*, (Philadelphia: W. D. Saunders Company, 1953), p. 337.

ports 73 per cent had premarital coitus by age 20.[4]   Findings by Hohman and Schaffner show that 80 per cent of single white soldiers age 21-28 reported non-marital coitus;[5] Burgess and Wallin state that of 580 husbands and 604 wives, most of whom were born after 1909, 68.8 per cent of the men and 47 per cent of the women had had premarital coitus.[6]   More recent surveys based on college student populations also indicate that premarital coitus is not uncommon.[7]   Professional counselors and other leaders in the field of marriage and the family are aware of the change in moral codes taking place in America as well as in some other countries.   The minister-counselor must face this problem realistically, not sentimentally, as he meets with it in his parochial work and in guiding young people.   The churches are aware of this problem as evidenced by proposals made by them regarding sex and family education.   (See Appendices I-IV.)

We may divide forced marriages into two classifications: (1) those couples who have known each other a long time, are deeply in love and plan to be married; (2) those couples who are going together somewhat casually, not yet sure whether they are in love or want to marry.   These latter present the biggest problem.

Couples in the former classification usually have guilt feelings, and their parents are generally upset because marriage plans have to be hurried up, changed radically, or dropped altogether—that is, the couple may simply get married by a civil official or some minister, usually not their own.   Of course, some of these couples never tell their parents about the pregnancy until sometime after the marriage.   The parents are often quite upset over this sudden turn of

[4] Alfred C. Kinsey et al., *Sexual Behavior in the Human Male*, (Philadelphia: W. D. Saunders Company, 1948), p. 550.

[5] Leslie B. Hohman and Bertram Schaffner, "The Sex Lives of Unmarried Men," *American Journal of Sociology*, LII (1947), © 1947 by the University of Chicago, p. 503.

[6] Ernest W. Burgess and Paul Wallin, *Engagement and Marriage*, (Philadelphia: J. B. Lippincott Company, 1953), p. 330.

[7] Robert R. Bell and Leonard Blumberg, "Courtship Intimacy and Religious Background," *Marriage and Family Living*, XXI, No. 4, (November 1959), p. 356.

events especially when there had been tentative plans for an elaborate wedding. There may be considerable friction between the young couple and the parents. Usually the *fait accompli* is accepted though the disappointment of the parents may remain for a long time. There are cases where it was never completely overcome. There is also disappointment on the part of the couple, especially the girl, who, having dreamed of a beautiful wedding, sees the dream suddenly shattered in a judge's dingy office.

Fortunate is the couple who seeks the counsel of their minister. For he can help them to have a simple but beautiful church wedding. He can help them with their guilt problem and disappointment so that they may start their life together on a religious basis and more easily win parental approval. Parents can accept the marriage much better when they, too, have received counseling in which they have had opportunity to express their feelings about the couple and urgency of the marriage. It is the counselor's part to lead all to an acceptance of the new situation, so that all may cooperate in making the marriage a happy one.

The tragedy of many forced marriages lies in the failure of the couple and/or their families to seek the counsel of the minister. The fear of exposure, or the shame that accompanies the premarital pregnancy causes the individuals concerned to conceal the real facts. But shame grows unless it is communicated. Talking about the concern diminishes the shame. Furthermore, the couple may concentrate so much on the evil of premarital coitus, that they cannot attain self-actualization in their marriage. So they are married secretly, or they run off and are married in another town, frequently by a civil officer or a "marrying parson" who cares little about the couple's future so long as he gets his fee. When the couple returns home, everything is done to cover up the reasons for the hasty or early marriage. Because of the circumstances of the marriage, people refrain from asking questions. In some cases they move to another town. Or the parents "disown" them, turn them out, and the couple goes off with not only guilt, but feelings of resentment toward their parents, making success of their mar-

riage all the more difficult. Every minister should let it be known
in every possible way that he will not condemn, lecture, or preach
to a couple being forced into marriage, but will do all in his power
to help them toward a happy marriage, consult with the unwed
mother about her problems, and help their parents to accept them
and cooperate in making the marriage a successful one.

Problems of the young couple. One of the problems of greatest
concern for the young couple being forced into marriage is, "What
will our parents say or do?"

If they do not know it, should they be told? This is not a question to be answered with a categorical "yes." First of all, it is a
decision the couple must make for themselves. Talking it out with
the counselor as they think it through will enable them to arrive at
a good decision. Also, talking out the whole matter in the presence
of the minister-counselor will relieve their feelings of shame, guilt,
fear, and anxiety. Some factors bearing on the question of telling
their parents will be (a) the time element of the pregnancy, whether
it is near the beginning or at the two or three month stage when it
would soon become obvious; (b) the relationship between the
young people and their parents, whether mutually trustful, close,
friendly, or distant, hostile; (c) the temperament of the parents:
their emotional stability in the face of crisis. To tell them might
be very cruel. They might be better able to accept it after the
marriage when faced with the *fait accompli* and become more accustomed to the new "in-laws." One mother, becoming very
upset when her daughter told her, said, "Why did you have to tell
me? I may have always suspected it, but now I know what an awful
thing you have done. At least you could have spared me knowing
it!" Should a couple tell their parents? Every case must be handled in the light of its own peculiar factors.

Young couples, being forced into marriage, even though engaged,
are faced with many other problems: livelihood, employment—if
parental support is withdrawn—education, guilt, anxieties, and
fears.

Let us consider the problem of guilt. Its degree of severity will depend very largely upon the rigidity of the moral code the individuals have been taught. Some couples believe they have committed the unpardonable sin and that God will punish them and may do so through the child. One girl was so distraught over her condition that she became nervous, lost weight, and on a pretext left home for a month in deep despair. She had been brought up in a Christian home, had always gone to Sunday School and church, but in a moment of intense passion she had violated her religious teaching on chastity and virginity and her parents' warnings. Another girl tried to have an abortion and talked of suicide. A long distance phone call to the boy brought him to her. They were deeply in love and soon married. Contrary to her expectations, her parents, according to a letter received from her later, showed remarkable understanding, accepted the situation and at last reports all were rejoicing over a fine baby.

These young people are frightened at marriage being suddenly thrust upon them. Many are unprepared in their planning and are emotionally immature. They know they have violated social and moral codes. They want to do the best thing, but need the counsel of a mature and skilled counselor. They need assurance for they feel so unsure. They need acceptance by someone who stands in a place of authority, such as their pastor. And if their parents reject them, the pastor is in a position to give them much of the moral support they need.

They should not be treated as "wicked" or "bad." They may be the same fine young people who grew up in the Church and received communion the Sunday before and since. They must not be made to feel that because their lives may have been damaged, they have been likewise ruined. It is true that they have been not only indiscreet in their intimacies or love-making, but have violated the Christian moral code. The fact of wrong-doing must not be minimized, but, at the same time, the minister is not the one to "cast the first stone." In all humility as a servant of God it is his duty to help the couple view their act objectively, evaluate it, repent and receive God's forgiveness, knowing that life is still full of great potentialities for them. After all, they may not be the only ones to bear the responsibility. The chances are they had no sex instruction, were not warned of the power of the sex drive. As one girl said, "Somehow it just happened so quick." There may have been no intention of wrong-doing. Girls are not taught constructively how to deal with the naturally aggressive male.

The unplanned marriage. The minister-counselor is approached by a couple being forced into marriage when there was no planning to marry and love had not developed. Here he is faced with a counseling situation which will draw upon all his resources as a pastor and counselor. The child must be considered; an unwanted child brought into a home without love will be terribly handicapped from the start. One solution is for the couple to marry so as to give the child a legitimate birth and then if by that time they do not love each other and do not wish to make the marriage permanent to seek a divorce. Many ministers would give support and sanction to such a conditional union. Another alternative would be for such couples to have only a civil ceremony, deferring the religious one until they might wish to make the marriage permanent. Love does sometime come into such marriages. An analogy would be marriages of "convenience" arranged by families without regard for the feelings of the boy and girl which take place in many countries. They are not all devoid of love. Love is known to develop in such marriages.

A couple thrown into this dilemma will have feelings of guilt, shame, and probably deep resentment against each other. They may have suffered greatly already from their fears and anxieties. Frustrated, they find it hard to think constructively. A wise, patient, understanding minister-counselor can be a real tower of strength to them in whatever direction they decide to resolve the problem. Of course, much of what I have already said about forced marriages will apply in helping work through their dilemma.

The parents' need for counseling. Sometimes, the most difficult people to deal with are the parents. Some parents are so unprepared for the girl's announcement of her pregnancy that they are dazed and bewildered. One parent said he could hardly believe what his wife was telling him about their daughter. He could not say anything.

It seemed like she was talking of someone else, maybe a story she had read. My mind was sort of blank. Then gradually I began to understand the awfulness of it. I remember for days I kept saying to myself, how can it be? But soon after she told me I became panicky. I guess that was my first reaction after I took it in. I now saw the family disgraced. Then I wondered would the man marry her, for I knew they were not in love. I was afraid—afraid for my daughter, afraid for my wife, and myself. She was our only child. Somehow, I never thought about this happening to people of our standing.

This man and his wife were relieved to know that they were not the first to face this problem. It helped them, too, that the minister did not condemn the daughter, nor them for any carelessness on their part. They began to see that what was most essential now was to think constructively, objectively, and to give their daughter the support she needed whether or not the man would marry her.

Counseling with parents can be of great help. Of course, they will not always seek counseling. Some will feel so embarrassed that they will avoid any meeting with the minister and stop coming to church for fear someone may say something about the marriage. But those who will come and talk it over are usually grateful for the opportunity to discuss it with their pastor knowing he will keep the matter confidential.[8] As they talk several things may become apparent:

1. Their child was not the first to be indiscreet.
2. Some parents admit that they themselves had engaged in pre-

---

[8] I have already commented on the importance of the minister "keeping his mouth shut." He should never disclose matters told him in confidence to anyone, not even his wife. If he makes it a practice not to relay confidential information to his wife, she can always honestly say to inquiries that she knows "nothing about it," and she will certainly have no information from her husband which someone may "pick" out of her. There are those who will try to pry out of him details about couples forced into marriage. To all such inquiries he must "know nothing" or have "no comment."

marital intercourse, and now their feelings of guilt and shame are expressed in condemnation of their child.   Of course, in condemning the child, they are really condemning themselves.   In some cases, this admission of premarital coitus on the part of the parents has great therapeutic value for them in relieving them of shame and guilt carried for many years.   Indeed, their "confession" may and often does lead to a new relationship between them and the Church.   For, having this load of shame and guilt lifted from them, they are free to move forward in the development of their personality as husband and wife, and of their potentials as Christian men and women.

3. They see that they are more afraid of the reflection upon them than they are anxious to make the marriage a success.

4. They are to think of the grandchild and that it is in no way responsible, but is entitled to a happy home and the love and care of grandparents.   In talking with a father and mother and after many tears, the first glimmer of a smile and of a hopeful future came as we began talking about the grandchild.   Soon their feeling of disgrace gave way to eager anticipation and planning for the baby. Parental love is deep, but self-love is deep, too, and if parents can see that they are not alone in their regret, but that more is involved than their feelings and that their children are not wicked, but the same children they have always loved, then they will usually come through to hope and expectation.

5. Another view that helps parents is that while normally in our culture intercourse follows marriage, this is not the case in all cultures; furthermore, that while we think of intercourse as the culmination of marriage, the marriage service is actually a blessing of the union.   The couple marry each other.   If they look upon their premarital relations as evidence of their love and its culmination, then they actually have already married each other.   The law by issuing a license legalizes it, and the Church by her service of Holy Matrimony blesses the union.

Does this indicate that there is, therefore, no reason for a couple to postpone intercourse until marriage?   By no means.   We still have the moral code and the mores of society to recognize, as well as the guilt and shame which follow those who violate them. The couple is in great need of forgiveness by God and by society as represented in the Christian fellowship for obviously they have violated their baptismal and confirmation vows to "keep God's holy will and commandments, and walk in the same all the days of my life." [9]

6. It is helpful to encourage parents to take a long look at the marriage. They may feel bitter now, but how will they feel a year from now? They may, in their anger, do something now that will make good relations with the young couple ever after extremely difficult. Some day they will want to enjoy their grandchildren, and, as old age comes on, they will want the companionship of this young couple who will then be mature. Indeed, they may become dependent on the couple; how much better then to forgive and accept the marriage.

7. Especially should they forgive now since the young couple needs them now more perhaps than they have ever or will ever need them. For they are under a cloud. They have their own problems of guilt; they probably did not want the child. They may be very immature and hence unprepared for the responsibilities of parenthood. And, if still in high school, as many are, what of their education—especially the boy? What trade will he learn? Would it be better to help him stay in school and continue with his chosen career? If he is forced to quit school, then his income the rest of his life may be in a very low bracket and the couple may face need all their lives. Many parents are quick to see that they should continue to support the young couple until the boy finishes his education and is launched on a career. Strong family solidarity is a great asset in such a case for the young couple needs forgiveness, acceptance, understanding, and love.

In forced marriages, then, it is obvious that the parents of the young people are in need of counseling as well as the couple.

[9] *Book of Common Prayer*, pp. 283, 293.

Divorced couples

Sarah fell in love with a divorced man who was much older than she. He had two children by his former spouse. They were in his custody. The girl and her parents were quite concerned about the proposed marriage. In consulting the minister-counselor, they stated their concerns: the cause of the divorce, which he was reluctant to discuss with them; the reaction of his children who were six and eight years of age, and how they would accept a stepmother; the age difference of about ten years; the attitude of his mother who had been living with him and caring for the children. These were all major concerns. Many interviews were held with the couple. The various problems were fully discussed. He realized the necessity for understanding the failure of his first marriage and went over the maladjustments very carefully. He discussed the first marriage with the girl and allayed her anxiety regarding it. They were finally married. A follow up after several years revealed a successful marriage.

Churches are giving more and more attention to the marriages of divorced persons. There is emphasis put upon the special needs of such persons for adequate counseling before the second marriage. The Church's attitude is not condemnatory for failure in the first marriage, but to help those seeking a second marriage to evaluate the failures in the first so that the second may be successful and a life-long Christian home established. The minister, dealing with such persons, must be very understanding and non-judgmental.

The Episcopal Church requires divorced persons seeking marriage to sign the Declaration of Intention with full understanding of its implications for the second marriage.

The Presbyterian Church in the United States stresses the importance of the redemptive Gospel of Christ as it relates to the "sin and failure" evident in the first marriage, causing the divorce, and emphasizes the forgiveness of God of those who show sufficient penitence. But the Presbyterian Church also raises the question as to whether or not the divorced person, having failed in one marriage, "should give prayerful thought to discover if God's vocation for them (divorced persons) is to remain unmarried." (See Appendix III.)

The United Lutheran Church in America points out "God's loving concern for man in his actual situation" and His readiness to deal with him according to his needs. But "the divorced person seeking remarriage must recognize his responsibility in the breakup of the former marriage. He must give evidence of repentance and have made an effort to overcome his limitations and failures. He must have forgiven his partner in the former marriage, and he and his intended spouse must give assurance that he will fulfill his obligations to those involved in his former marriage. The divorced person must give evidence of his Christian faith by his witness in the church and must have received adequate counsel and training in preparation for marriage. He must be prepared to undertake the full responsibilities of marriage in dependence upon God." (See Appendix IV.)

The United Lutheran Church in America notes above one factor that other churches seem to have overlooked: the need for the divorced person to face up to and fulfill his or her obligations to those involved in the former marriage. These obligations, as for example, support of children in the former marriage, or regular visits to and from children of that marriage, often cause arguments and resentment in the second marriage. These matters relating to the former marriage should be fully discussed and an understanding reached in premarital counseling.

The importance of premarital counseling before a second marriage for either partner lies in the opportunity, it seems, to examine the first marriage so that the next one may not end also in divorce. A divorced person may be fully aware of his failures in the marriage, as one woman said, "I will not make those mistakes again!" She referred to her lack of consideration for her husband's sex needs, her failure to assume her role as a housewife, and her "bossiness."

The marriages of children of divorced couples are apt also to end in divorce. Divorce tends to beget divorce. Therefore, in counseling the divorced individual of divorced parents, it is necessary to consider the psychological factors in both marriages. What went wrong and why? Otherwise, the second marriage, or third, or whatever number it may be, may end also in divorce.

One young woman whose parents had been divorced discussed freely what she knew about her parents, her own reactions to them and to the divorce and said, "I am determined that my marriage will be a success. I know what divorce has done to me and I do not intend that it shall happen to my children."

Of course, there are ministers who will not marry divorced persons under any circumstances, but I do not see this as a reason for not counseling with the individuals involved in a second marriage. They need help in forming the new marriage; and whether or not the minister marries them, they are very likely to get married anyway. Usually these individuals are older than those marrying for the first time. One or the other may be reluctant about premarital counseling and even refuse to come for it. In that case it is possible to do what one can for the other one. If that be the divorced one, all the better.

In counseling with a divorced person, the field may be quite wide and varied. The factors that caused the breakup of the former marriage may lead into psychological areas involving homosexuality, casual extramarital sex relations, alcoholism and drug addiction, or immaturity, causing the average minister-counselor to feel inadequate. As in all such cases, he should not hesitate to send the person to a professional marriage counselor, psychologist, or psychiatrist.

The Presbyterian Church in the United States gives the following direction to its ministers regarding the preparation for marriage of divorced persons:

When a Christian who has been divorced applies to a minister for remarriage, the minister's chief concern shall be the applicant's present fitness of heart and life for the intended marriage. The supreme test of this fitness should be one's honest purpose to profit from past experiences and to plan and work for a Christian home on soundly spiritual foundations. Careful attention should also be given to the applicant's psychological readiness for a new marriage experience. If the applicant has been clearly and grossly wronged by a previous mate, this fact may incline the Church to allow and sanction the remarriage without further question, but the mere fact of having been wronged will not necessarily mean that the applicant understands fully the spiritual demands of marriage and holds to a high and serious purpose to make the coming marriage Christian. The minister, therefore, shall take care to be as fully satisfied on the latter point as on the first. On the other hand, if the applicant has been clearly at fault in the break-up of the earlier marriage, or is found even to be chiefly at fault, the mere fact of previous guilt (however grievous) should not be held as a rigid and final disqualification for remarriage under the auspices and with the sanction of the Church. Here, too, the minister shall weigh, as of paramount importance, the quality of the applicant's present faith, contrition and purpose, being mindful always of the infinite mercy of God and careful never to hold against any honest child of God a sin which God Himself may have forgiven and put behind Him forever. In a word, in all cases where remarriage is sought, the minister's decision shall turn not so much on what the applicant has done but rather on what this person by God's grace has now become, and what, with God's help, he (or she) honestly intends and hopes to do in the future.

The Session of each church may appoint a committee to advise with the minister in all cases where divorced persons make application for remarriage. The minister may seek the advice of this committee and after a careful investigation on the basis of our Church's Standards and a conscientious consideration of all pertinent facts may approve or decline the request. Normally, the applicants should appear before the committee to state their case and declare their intention to establish a Christian home.

The Presbytery may appoint a committee on remarriage to which may be referred cases upon which the minister or the Session feels it may be better qualified to render a decision.

In all instances of the remarriage of divorced persons the officiating minister shall, before solemnizing the marriage, seek definite assurance that the attitude of the parties toward their marriage is in accordance with the fundamental doctrines of our Church. [See Appendix III.]

The problem of children in second marriages will be considered under the next section on widows and widowers.

Widows and widowers

Widows and widowers also need premarital counseling before they enter upon another marriage. Whether the previous marriage was a happy one or not, there are serious problems to be considered. Can the partner who may have never been married before accept the experiences of the other partner's love life with someone else in years gone by? If there are children still in the home, can the other partner accept them and love them? Will the children accept another in mother's or father's place? If one has never married before, can he or she suddenly take on a ready-made family and adjust to them? Some of the most unhappy situations brought to a counselor develop out of these marriages.

Not infrequently, children resent bitterly what they interpret as the intruder who comes into the home and takes "Daddy's" or "Mama's" place. The newcomer does not understand the psychological problem of the stepchild and may retaliate by rejecting the child, or by showing favoritism if his children are also involved, or by oppressive action. Where older children are involved they may strongly oppose the marriage and from the beginning of the courtship show hostility toward the other partner. This may be particularly severe if there is any threat to any inheritance.

Every minister has found himself in the midst of the tragedy of a family in a second marriage being torn apart by inheritance squabbles when either parent died. Much unhappiness might be prevented if the two parties to a second marriage would draw up wills before the marriage with the full knowledge and consent of the children, provided they are mature enough to understand the situation. Then the children know that the newcomer into the family will not be a threat to the inheritance. Where the furniture and other possessions are to be mixed after the wedding, it is wise for each to label, or carefully list, his furniture because often there may be sentimental, if not monetary value attached to certain pieces which ultimately should go to the side of the family from which they came. If not labelled or listed, time may cause confusion as to which heirs they belong.

Widows and widowers need to know what they may expect and what measures can be taken to lessen the dangers to the marriage.

If the woman has never been married, she must be able to accept the fact that the husband has loved another, perhaps had children by her and that, consequently, a big part of his life is inseparably connected with someone else and always will be. She must see that love objectively and accept it as a part of her husband. To expect him never to talk about the first wife, never to look at her picture is hardly reasonable. A wise woman will encourage her husband to talk about his first wife, not for comparing the present one with her, but to help him to accept the present one in her place. Certainly, it would be unwise for either partner to bring up the first love with such remarks as "John never treated me as you do." Or "Mary would never have said that."

Helping a couple to understand their emotions about the past and present marriage relationship is of inestimable value to them in the premarital counseling.

A young war widow with four small children was planning a marriage with a bachelor of 38. The woman had never considered many of the factors involved in such a marriage: How would he get along with the four children? What would his reactions be when he wanted to be alone with his wife, but there would be "all these children hanging onto her skirt"? Bachelors, as well as spinsters, often have very definite ideas about how children should behave and how parents should control them. Was this man to look upon her children as "brats of another man" or identify them with the woman he loved and see her as their mother and his wife and sweetheart? Would he be willing before marriage to read and learn about the care of children and how to be a father to them? Could he be objective enough before marriage to see himself in the role of father?   Would he be able to understand their love for their deceased father and their feeling toward the stepfather and try patiently to win them over and show that he could love them too?

We went over these and many other problems with the wife, for the man was not available. There was the problem of sex, for example. Would she be able to give herself completely as a sex partner when she held cherished memories of her first husband? As she was going to his city to be married and live, a marriage counselor was recommended to them in that city, and they agreed to go to him.[10]   She wrote later that they had had an appointment with the marriage counselor and were very grateful for the referral.

It is my general experience that persons planning a second marriage welcome the opportunity to talk with a minister-counselor.

Wide differences in age

Another class of marriages, less frequently encountered, but in need of premarital counseling, is that in which the age difference is great enough to present serious problems of adjustment.

Why does an attractive young woman marry a man many years older?   What factors should the counselor look for in this proposed marriage?

Here the minister, if he has been in the same parish for a number of years, especially if the girl has grown up in his church, has a special advantage over the professional counselor because the minister may have a good deal of knowledge about the girl's family. He may have observed influences upon the girl when she was a child.   For example, he may know that her father was distant toward her, never gave her the warm affection she craved from him,

---

[10] The American Association of Marriage Counselors, Inc., 104 E. 40th St., New York 16, N. Y. will be glad to furnish the names of reputable marriage counselors.

and now in marriage she is seeking a father substitute in whom her childhood longings may at last be satisfied. She must understand her desires toward her fiance and differentiate between him and her father so that the former will not come to occupy the psychological space left vacant by her father and cease to be her sweetheart.

Of course, at times every husband and every wife must play the role of father and mother, respectively, to the other spouse. There are times when everyone wants to experience again the comfort, understanding, and sympathy of one's parents. There is a mother in every wife, a father in every husband. But marital maladjustment comes when one or the other spouse allows the parental relationship to substitute for the romantic relationship of sweetheart and wife, sweetheart and husband.

Here lies a real danger as age differences increase. A man who marries a girl many years his junior can meet, to a degree, the demands of a youthful wife, provided she, herself, is mature. A child wife is difficult under any circumstances. Jealousy and suspicion come easily to the husband. His fear of losing her love may create an impossible situation.

But the man who marries a woman several years his senior will find many problems in companionship and sex. Each of them must have a clear understanding of the other's needs and how best to meet them.

A couple in this category came for premarital counseling. There was a difference of eight years in ages, the woman being the senior. At the time the man was 19. Her family was bitterly opposed to the marriage. The boy was still in college and had no income except what his parents sent him, which was barely sufficient for his expenses. The girl had a secretarial job. They planned for her to work until he finished college. In spite of all opposition from both families, they persisted in the marriage plans including a large church wedding. In the premarital counseling, both parties reviewed their childhood and relations with their parents. It was quite clear that each was seeking to meet unsatisfied childhood needs for parental affection; each felt it to be found in the other.

During the counseling, which extended over several weeks, their understanding of the dynamics that seemed to be propelling them toward each other seemed to enrich their courtship and deepen their love. They have now been married several years and have children. Their marriage is a happy one. Both families have accepted it and have not interfered.

There are many combinations in age differences. As, for example, the man who marries a girl twenty years his junior; the elderly widower, with a family, who marries a young wife the age of his elder daughter; the woman who marries a man several years her junior, or a young widower with children. All such couples need premarital counseling to help them enter marriage with good self-understanding and understanding of the other partner. Generally speaking, the cards are stacked against them, as evidenced by divorce statistics. But many of these marriages do turn out successfully and more of them would if premarital counseling were available to them.

Now it should be said that older men—men of 60 who marry women of 40 or 50—seem to be able to make the marriage successful. Perhaps because a woman of that age, especially if never before married, can adjust to the ways of the older man and cater to his whims. One woman who married a bachelor in his forties said she knew she could not change his ways but she, being the younger, would adjust her ways to his. They have a happy companionship and a successful marriage.

Marriages between different nationalities and/or races

Interracial marriages are much more common since the war. Among military personnel we find many marriages with foreigners. Interracial is hardly the correct word to describe these marriages, because many of them are not actually interracial but international, if we accept the present anthropological division of mankind into three races—Caucasoid, Mongoloid and Negroid.

The special problems pertaining to these marriages involve national traditions, language, child training, and religion.

Chaplains in military service are more apt to be consulted in regard to proposed marriages in this category than the average parochial minister.

Here it is important that each partner make a determined effort to learn before marriage as much as possible about the national traditions of the countries involved, and there should be a willingness in each to respect these traditions and accept them insofar as may be necessary to insure marital happiness. Obviously, a Japanese bride coming to America would be unable to follow many traditions of her native land. In this case, the husband must learn to appreciate his wife's yearning for the familiar ways of her native place and not chide her for it. One Japanese bride was disappointed in coming to the United States because there was no temple or shrine where she might worship. She decided to become a Christian, but her husband had no interest in the Church, and from what she had learned of Christianity no one seemed to be living as Christians. However, she did finally, after much explaining on the part of a minister, decide to be baptized.

Another couple, in which case the man was a foreigner, had trouble with child discipline. The husband wanted to follow a stern system of regimentation and instant obedience with "clicking of heels"; whereas, the wife wished to rear the children according to modern psychology. The children clearly showed in their behavior this conflict of authority.

Marriages between Protestant and Greek Orthodox also present serious problems, especially if the latter is a staunch member of his church and the family moves exclusively in a Greek community. The Protestant will have much to learn and long services to endure.

Couples with socio-economic differences

Certainly, experience seems to indicate that couples who marry in their own cultural group have a better chance of success than those who cross cultural lines, and the same applies in many cases to economic lines. However, we read sometimes of the Cinderellas who marry wealthy men and are capable of meeting the situation and proving themselves successful wives and homemakers.

In regard to cultural factors, education is one of the most important. If the girl is a college graduate and the man is not, it will be easy for friction to develop between them because of her "superior" knowledge and attempts to "educate" him. One husband became furious with his college-bred wife who was continually trying to educate him. A girl preparing for marriage brought a similar complaint against her fiance. She said their only arguments were over her poor, countrified English. She had had a business course in high school and he had received an A.B. degree. She said he would laugh at her grammar and use of words. He would stop her in the midst of a sentence and tell her the correct construction or supply a better word. Her fiance also came from a "fashionable" family, whereas hers was a "dirt farmer" family. There seemed no doubt of the sincerity of their love. He insisted he wanted to help her so he would not be embarrassed when in his home and among his friends. She faced up to the reality of this problem, was helped to talk about her family and admitted to herself that there was a cultural difference, but also that with her husband's help and understanding she could improve her English and learn the social graces he felt were so important. Also her husband was encouraged to talk about the cultural difference. He was reluctant to do this at first because he felt it would be disloyal to his fiance. When he finally did talk, he began to see her cultural deficiencies objectively and ways in which he could help her without belittling her. She, also, came to see that her desire to improve herself could be strengthened by her fiance's interest and help. Books and private tutoring were suggested, which were easy now for her to accept since she, too, saw the situation objectively. If this couple had married without the benefit of premarital counseling, the marriage would undoubtedly have been a very unhappy one.

In these marriages the in-laws are apt to be very troublesome. It is very important, if at all possible, that the counselor should talk with the in-laws, particularly the mothers-in-law. Because women seem more sensitive about these cultural differences than men. The mother who belongs to the lower cultural stratum may seek to disparage the son-in-law and his family by looking for weaknesses in other areas, such as personal habits, or by calling his family snobbish. Also, the culturally superior family may actually act snobbish toward the other or may ostentatiously flaunt their culture and/or wealth before them. Furthermore, the in-laws may criticize the husband or wife and make life very miserable for them. Certainly, couples should be agreed that if there is any criticism of either by either family that each must "take up" for the other.

A young bride returning from her first visit, after marriage, to her husband's home came for counseling. She broke down in tears as she told how his family had criticized her and her husband had sided with them. She felt rejected and lonely. This couple had not had premarital counseling. Their backgrounds were quite different. She was reared in a city and had traveled widely. He came from a small rural community. When the husband came for counseling, it was plain that one of his problems was divided loyalty—loyalty to his family vying with loyalty to his wife's family. He felt that loyalty to his wife meant acceptance of her family as superior and the rejection of his as inferior. It required several interviews for him to see that there was much in his family to be proud of, and that it was not really a question of choosing one or the other, but of incorporating the best of both families into the new family.

In premarital counseling we have opportunity to help couples understand the importance of giving each other mutual support in the presence of their families. This is one meaning of "forsaking all others."

In this connection, I point out to couples that up to the present each has been sailing under the flag of his own family. They have been loyal to the family and the traditions and customs for which it stands. Now, in marriage, they are to raise their own flag, to which they must be loyal and around which will gather the combined and modified traditions and customs each will contribute to this new relationship. In order to be loyal to each other, they must forswear allegiance to their respective family traditions and customs. One can not serve under two flags at the same time and be equally loyal to both. "Forsaking all others" means cutting former family relationships so that a strong union may be formed between husband and wife.

Once couples of different cultural and economic levels understand this and accept it, they see their home-to-be in a different light, and realize that each has much to contribute to it, and that in reality a truly successful home reflects the best in the traditions and customs brought to it.

Couples with religious differences

There are two categories of religiously mixed marriages which need to be dealt with in particular: marriages between Protestants and Roman Catholics and marriages between members of different Protestant churches. We might also classify marriages between members of liturgical churches, such as Episcopal, Lutheran, Roman Catholic, and non-liturgical churches, Baptist, Methodist, Congregational.

In premarital counseling, the minister has an unusual opportunity to help the member of another communion to express his feelings about religion and his church and see them objectively: provided, and this must be emphasized, he feels safe in doing so. That is, he is confident that the minister is not going to try to convert him to his church. A counselor must be neutral here. If he uses the counseling sessions for evangelistic purposes or to expound his church's doctrine, his usefulness as a counselor is over. However, he can and should answer questions honestly and fairly.

The Church should be a uniting factor in every Christian marriage, and the more couples share in common, the more stable the mar-

riage will be.   Therefore, couples should unite in the same church.
Which church should be left to them.   They may attend each
other's church alternately until they decide on one or the other, or
on a third church.

In fairness, each would do well to learn something about the
other's church.   This can be and often is done before marriage.
It may result in a change of church before marriage.   This is also
good because then they can be married in their church, rather
than in the woman's, as is customary.

Generally speaking, the wife should join her husband's church.
In our Hebrew-Christian tradition, the father is "the priest-of-the-
home" and is, therefore, responsible for the religion of the home
and of the religious training of the children.   It seems that men
are more apt to maintain interest in their own church than if, without deep convictions, they change to another.   There are many
nominal Christians whom we must counsel for marriage.   Some will
never be more than nominal, but to uproot and transplant them to
another church may mean the severance of all religious ties.

If one partner is keenly interested in his church and the other
only nominally interested in his, then it would seem best for the
latter to joint the church of the former.   Though this cannot be
laid down as a rule.   A man who had no interest in his church
until he married and his wife became a member, soon became an
enthusiastic churchgoer and worker.

When we come to marriages between Protestants and Roman
Catholics, we find the problem more serious.   Some churches, such
as the Episcopal and Methodist, discourage such marriages.   (See
Appendices I and II.)   But they do take place, and eventually
every Protestant minister is called upon for counseling a member
of his church who has fallen in love with a Roman Catholic.   It is
wise that ministers speak to their young people occasionally about
marriages outside their faith to apprise them of the possibility that
serious marital conflicts may arise as a result of divergent religious
beliefs.   Several good books deal with this and related problems

and should be made accessible to young people.   (See Bibliography.)

Just as in the case of marriages between Christians and Jews and between Protestants and members of the Greek Orthodox Churches, those who fall in love with Roman Catholics should be fully informed about the other's religion, its requirements of its members and of the Protestant as a married partner.

Summary

I have attempted to present in this chapter suggestions for the premarital counseling of couples marrying under special circumstances.   These people are in need of understanding as they attempt marriage in the face of trying conditions.   In many cases the "strikes" are against them.   However, their marriages have a better chance of success if the minister-counselor will seek, through empathy and understanding, to give them support as they work toward laying the foundation for a happy marriage.

IV

ESSENTIAL AREAS
FOR CONSIDERATION

7

Personality needs

Effective marriage counseling depends upon a certain degree of knowledge of the personality factors involved in marital adjustment. Premarital counseling also takes account of these factors. By the time a man and woman have come to a marriageable age, they are the product of all that has contributed to the development of their personalities from the prenatal stage. By way of illustration, we may schematically represent a person as a cone-shaped receptacle formed by biological, psychological and sociological influences into which is being poured continually all his experiences. Thus at any age a cross section gives a picture in behavior patterns which is the sum of all that has gone into the forming of this particular individual to that point in his development. When a man and woman are united in marriage, an interplay of all these forces in each individual takes place. In order for them to work together as a team, each must be flexible enough to give and take in the stress and strain of the interpersonal relationship that comes with marriage.

What, then, are some of the factors that make up the individual?

All of us have needs to be met. There are primary needs such as hunger, thirst, and sex. These needs are obvious and will not concern us at this point, except to say that when they are not met, they have a profound psychological effect upon us, and may cause us to do things we would not do otherwise.

In our society, people are not concerned as individuals so much with physical needs as with psychological needs. These latter needs are of prime importance in marriage and those who seek to do premarital counseling must be aware of them and how they may be met, and of the results of their frustrations.

Five levels of needs

Maslow presents five levels of needs which he arranges in a hierarchy, from the most basic physiological drives to higher-level psychological needs which represent the higher development of the personality.[1] The basic physiological drives must be satisfied if the individual is to direct his energies toward gratifying his psychological needs which are basic to the enhancement of the personality.

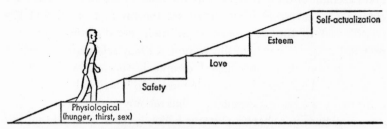

Maslow's hierarchy of needs[2]

[1] James C. Coleman, *Abnormal Psychology and Modern Life* (© 1950, 1956 by Scott, Foresman and Company, Chicago), p. 68.
[2] A. H. Maslow, *Motivation and Personality*, (New York: Harper & Brothers, 1954), Chap. 5. The drawing above is based on Maslow's article, "A Theory of Human Motivation," *Psychological Review*, L (1943) pp. 370-396. Used by permission.

Maslow's hierarchy envisions these five levels of needs.   Only as our needs on the "lower," more prepotent, levels are satisfied do we seek satisfaction and expression of our "higher," less prepotent, needs and drives.[3]

Coleman lists the following among major needs which are essential to the development of a wholesome personality: security, adequacy, affection, social approval, self-esteem and reality testing.[4]

Safety

This factor is evident when physiological needs are satisfied. The child must find security in his home environment if he is to reach toward the higher level needs.   Quarreling, physical assault, name calling, separation, divorce, or death within the family may be particularly terrifying to the child, especially if he is roughly handled or threatened.   Children who are reared in an unthreatening, loving family do not ordinarily feel insecure and act frightened when a life situation changes suddenly.

In such children the danger reactions are apt to come mostly to objects or situations that adults would consider dangerous.   The healthy, normal, fortunate adult in our culture is largely satisfied in his safety needs. . . . Some neurotic adults in our society are, in many ways, like the unsafe child in their desire for safety, although in the former it takes on a somewhat special appearance.   Their reaction is often to unknown, psychological dangers in a world that is perceived to be hostile, overwhelming and threatening.   Such a person behaves as if a great catastrophe were almost always impending, i.e., he is usually responding as if to an emergency. . . .

The neurotic individual may be described with great usefulness as a grown-up person who retains his childish attitude toward the world. That is to say, a neurotic adult may be said to behave as if he were actually afraid of a spanking, or of his mother's disapproval, or of being

[3] James C. Coleman, *Abnormal Psychology and Modern Life* (© 1950, 1956 by Scott, Foresman and Company, Chicago), p. 69.
[4] *Ibid.*, p. 100.

abandoned by his parents, or having his food taken from him.   It is as if his childish attitude of fear and threat reaction to a dangerous world had gone underground, and untouched by the growing up and learning processes, were now ready to be called out by any stimulus that would make a child feel endangered and threatened.[5]

However, as Maslow states, not all neurotic individuals feel unsafe.   A thwarting of the affection and esteem needs in a person who generally feels safe may produce a neurosis.

Security

The belief that one's environment is stable and not subject to arbitrary and pernicious change is necessary for steady and normal development.   To know that those who make up one's constellation of persons—parents, spouse, children, business associates, and friends—will be consistently favorable, and not given to unusual, distrustful, or explosive reactions gives one a sense of security.

A young woman whose father drank excessively approached marriage with much fear and anxiety, for she had never experienced any security in her home.   There was never enough money for necessities; the father was continually changing jobs; the mother left him time and again taking the children with her, and always leaving for the last time; the girl was frequently embarrassed before her friends by her father's actions.   It was important that her intended husband understand this unmet need for security in his wife-to-be, and know that it must be met by him in providing her with a consistently stable environment.

As the young woman came to understand her own problems of insecurity, she learned to discriminate between her father and fiance.   As the fiance did not drink and was a quiet, stable person, she began to look forward to a marriage in which she now had confidence that she would find security.

Unconsciously, individuals transfer their feelings of love, fear, and hate from significant persons in their childhood environment to

[5] Maslow, *Motivation and Personality*, pp. 87-88.

later acquaintances; also, emotional reactions to certain traumatic situations may become attached to later similar situations. A wife may come to see her husband as her father; or a husband, his wife as his mother. A drinking husband, with a resulting environment of unemployment, may throw the wife back into an insecure home environment she experienced as a child. In order that these emotional reactions of childhood may not be carried into the marriage relationship, the individual must learn to discriminate or differentiate between the significant figures and situation of the past and those of the present.

Discrimination in premarital counseling as a psychological process is essential to an individual who has been closely attached to one parent or the other, or who may have suffered some traumatic experience as a child at the hands of either parent or of some other individuals resulting in a generalization regarding all men or women. Without discrimination this generalization may come to include the future husband or wife. Talking out such attachments or traumatic experiences will enable one to realize that the other partner is not the person who affected adversely one's behavior pattern but is actually one's sweetheart and soon to be one's beloved spouse.

The recovery of memories is not only a barometer of progress indicating the ego's increased ability to face repressed emotional situations; it has the additional therapeutic value of helping a person to learn how to discriminate between the past and present situation. For example, a person's early manifestations of aggressiveness have been intimidated by a father who required complete submissiveness from his son. As a result (following the principle of "spreading" or generalization of emotional reactions) the person has become inhibited in all situations in which he faces a person of authority. By reviving past emotional reactions toward the father, we enable the person to develop the power to differentiate between the original childhood situation and his present status. He will then realize that he is no longer helpless and that he can afford to resist the oppressive attitude of others.[6]

[6] Franz Alexander and Thomas M. French, *Psychoanalytic Therapy*, (New York: The Ronald Press Company, 1946), p. 21.

Love

To love and be loved is basic to psychological health. A Christian marriage is based upon a mutual love between husband and wife. But, there are individuals who have never received love and affection in such a way as to have learned to show them. Affection, which is one of the concrete evidences of love, is learned by having been experienced as an infant and on through childhood and adolescence.

Affection must be sincere. It must be on the basis of what one is, not what one does. There must be no ulterior motive tied to affection such as receiving gifts, being taken out, making more money, or being "good." Affection is not to be bought or sold. Love's power to redeem, strengthen, and encourage in marriage lies in its ability to be affectionate toward another because he or she is one's spouse and a part of one's own self. "Husbands should love their wives as their own bodies. He who loves his wife loves himself. For no man ever hates his own flesh, but nourishes and cherishes it, as Christ does the Church, because we are members of his body." [7] Affection between a Christian couple goes far beyond what might be expected of the non-Christian because the former sees in the spouse one like himself: a member of the Body of Christ, one whom Christ loved not for what he did, but for what he is— a child of God.

The ability to love and show affection is very important to marital happiness. In fact, it is essential in overcoming feelings of insecurity, for a person who feels insecure may have much of his fear and anxiety allayed by a loving and affectionate spouse.

In many of the cases involving unhappy couples who have consulted me about their marriages one spouse has complained of lack of love and a show of affection on the part of the other spouse. When the spouse was consulted, it was discovered that he or she

[7] Ephesians 5:28-30

had never learned in the parental home how to express love through affection. Remarks of counselees are common such as, "My family is not an affectionate one." "I never saw my parents kiss, except in a perfunctory sort of way." One young woman said in pre-marital counseling, "I have no recollection of ever seeing my parents kiss or even embrace. My father never kissed me or held me on his lap. He was always indifferent to me as well as to my mother." Obviously, she had a very warped idea of affection between husband and wife, and had she married without the benefit of premarital counseling would probably have found an affectionate relationship with her husband difficult to maintain.

This is not to convey the impression that all who have been denied affectionate experiences of love in the home will make an unhappy marriage. There are many people who, because of their own inner resources and drives, become affectionate. The point is that pre-marital counseling gives the counselor an opportunity to help the affection-starved individual to understand his needs; to learn to give expression to them; to seek, in turn, the satisfaction of those needs from the other partner, and, of course, to help the other partner understand the affectional needs of the spouse and how to supply those needs in a kind and considerate way.

Esteem

Every individual wants to be proud of himself. This applies to the normal and the abnormal. In fact, what is abnormal is but an irrational or exaggerated use of the ego-defense mechanism. Each of us will defend his self-esteem to the last "man" with all the ego defense available to us. We are rightly proud of ourselves. He who does not respect himself will hardly respect others; indeed, he who does not love himself will not love his neighbor. Self-esteem is one of our most basic psychological needs.

How many parents humiliate their children by calling them names, or by insulting them through corporal punishment, especially slapping. Perhaps a parent's hardest job is to find adequate ways of punishing or disciplining a child without lowering his self-esteem.

One of my most painful pastoral calls was in a home where there was a young girl of about 14 years of age. It was my first visit. The family was a transient one and strangers to me. The girl was present throughout the visit. She was shy, held her head down, and seldom looked up at anyone. After a few casual greetings and remarks with the parents I addressed the girl, asking how she liked our school. On the table her books lay open before her. She was on the point of answering when her father said, "She is too stupid to learn anything. She won't study. She can't read. She never remembers anything. She brings home nothing but low grades." Unprepared for this explosion, I tried to find some words to relieve the girl's embarrassment. But the mother then added to the father's verbal whipping before a stranger. The girl made no reply, and only hung her head lower.

Is that an exaggeration? What of the frequent remarks of parents: He's a bad boy. He's a baby. He's clumsy. He fouled the ball. The recounting of errors the child made in a game may amount to ridicule and belittling of the child. Then when children retaliate by doing things which embarrass the parents, who is to blame?

What of these same children when they grow up and enter the marriage relationship? Sometimes, they use the same methods to try to control their spouses. Sometimes, they feel that their self-esteem can be boosted only by tearing down the spouse.

Ned, 35, had had a few drinks and was feeling very depressed and lonely when he came to the office late one evening by appointment. His story was like others I had heard of a wife's criticism of her husband for not achieving the success she had hoped he would gain. Recently, he had lost another job in a series of dismissals for drinking and inefficiency. Now, he had begun heavy drinking with the result that his wife had "shut the door on me, and said she was through."

It later became possible for me to see his wife. We went over her husband's training. He had a college degree in his profession. Prior to their marriage he had done well and had a bright future. But she was socially ambitious and impatient. She decided to "whip" her husband into a successful career by using ridicule and by comparing him unfavorably with others, thinking he would become so ashamed that he would never rest until he excelled his contemporaries. But she had not figured on, indeed she did not understand, the simple dynamics of self-esteem. She so lowered his self-esteem that she undermined his self-confidence and finally convinced him that he was a failure, and this he soon became. Unable to hold a position, unable to meet his family needs, he sought escape in alcohol.

Fortunately, this had only just started. His wife found that she loved him, and he loved her. When she discovered her mistake, she received him back, and began following a few simple suggestions to help him regain his self-esteem. She praised him sincerely for whatever he did well, such as mowing the lawn. She expressed pride in whatever job he had, also gave him love and affection. Later she was surprised at his ability to rise in his profession. He, too, came to reevaluate his ability, took stock of his resources and gradually regained his self-confidence. They are now a happy family, even possessing the material things she once tried to force him into acquiring. Liquor never became a problem because with the return of his self-esteem and his wife's understanding there was nothing from which to escape. This couple had not had the advantage of premarital counseling in which the wife would have become aware of the importance of approval as a sound means of undergirding self-esteem and self-confidence in her husband.

This case has been presented in order to show how important it is in premarital counseling to help couples not to fall into the old trap of trying to shame people into success. The ego is strengthened by any sincere praise and is quick to recognize appreciation. It is essential that couples understand the part self-esteem plays in our interpersonal relationships.

Self-acceptance

Although this might have been treated along with self-esteem, because of its importance, I wish to single it out by treating it separately. Many people find it difficult to accept themselves as they are. This does not mean, of course, that they should be content with their shortcomings. It means rather to understand one's abilities and develop them to their fullest, while at the same time being realistic about one's limitations. Children are sometimes propelled along lines of endeavor for which they have no ability or potentialities. Because a father was a famous football player does not mean that his son will necessarily become one. But the father who pushes his son into a role which he is incapable of fulfilling creates in him a sense of failure with corresponding anxiety for not having come up to his father's expectations, thereby making him unacceptable to himself.

Such a boy needs to know that his seeming failure was not due to any lack of courage or stamina, but to a physical condition or lack of aptitude; therefore, he must accept himself as unfitted for football, or perhaps any sports, but capable of excelling in other activities. He needs also to know that his father understands this and accepts him just as fully as if he had athletic prowess. To be accepted for what one is, in the full light of one's weaknesses and failures, and to accept one's self, are prime steps in good mental health which play a vital part in marital adjustment.

Severe and continued self-recrimination over wasted opportunities or past unethical behavior plays havoc with feelings of security and adequacy and may predispose the individual to fear even success because of the inevitable failure and punishment which he vaguely senses in the offing. As a result of this orientation, he is also apt to become reaction-sensitive and to search back through his past life, locating and exaggerating his failures and misdeeds as his guilt-motivated self-recrimination and self-blame progress.

It is obvious that a healthy personality adjustment and severe self-devaluation are mutually incompatible, and one of the most important and difficult aspects of psycho-therapy is to help the individual to understand and accept himself as a worthwhile person. Only in this way can he avoid the hurt and achieve the emotional security, spontaneity, and normal, healthy attitudes conducive to mature self-realization. And, as Fromm has pointed out, the individual who dislikes himself is incapable of liking other people.[8]

Adequacy

To be self-reliant and feel adequate to meet the demands of life are important bases for marital adjustment. For marriage is for adults and carries with it large responsibilities. Young people who have been overprotected by either parent, or both, and not allowed to make decisions, face marriage either with a feeling of inadequacy or irresponsibility. The overprotected individual is never sure of himself, and is all too ready to shift responsibility for his actions upon others. In marriage he may prove to be indecisive in critical issues, or he may be the playboy who laughs off important matters.

Therefore, it is important for the counselor to know a good deal about how the man and woman planning marriage were taught to shoulder responsibilities and make decisions.

Parents of a lovely, capable young woman of 21 came to ask me what I could do to stop the marriage of their daughter, with whom I had begun premarital counseling. I listened to their arguments: "She is so immature, really only a child. She knows nothing about making a home, or cooking. She just does not know anything. You must stop her. Until she went off to college she never even bought her own clothes. We had to make all her decisions for her. She is our only child. She has never really grown up."

I had already learned from the daughter how overprotective her parents had been and that she herself welcomed college as a way

[8] James C. Coleman, *Abnormal Psychology and Modern Life* (© 1950, 1956 by Scott, Foresman and Company, Chicago), p. 126.

out from under their domination. In college she began to enjoy freedom and to make decisions, buy her own clothes, choose her friends. She soon determined not to return home after graduation but seek a position in another city. She did. And when I began counseling with her she had made a place for herself, held a very responsible position, and was very mature in her planning for her marriage.

I pointed this out to her parents who listened "open-mouthed" as though I surely could not be describing their daughter. The young woman was now faced with her greatest decision, for her parents, in spite of what I tried to do, refused to let her go on with her marriage plans "at least for the present," they said. She realized that if the future was to be hers she would have to cut now the parental apron string, painful though it be for them, and for her, too, because she was a sensitive girl and did not want needlessly to hurt her parents.

Later, she told them that she was a mature woman, knew whom she wished to marry and would marry the boy regardless of their consent, that they could cooperate and help to make it a happy marriage or not, as they wished, but the marriage would go on as planned. The parents cried, accused her of not loving them, pointed out all they had done for her, and that she was all they had. The girl stood her ground. The wedding took place with the full cooperation of the parents, and the marriage has been a successful one.

I can only conjecture what might have happened had the girl not come for premarital counseling. She would not have understood her own rebellion and striving for independence. She would have defied her parents and embittered them, and begun marriage under a cloud. Unless the parents had been brought into the counseling process, they would not have been prepared for her insistence on her rights and might have rejected her in retaliation. The parents were able now to discover in part the reasons for their overprotectiveness and began to find a new relationship between themselves, while the girl learned a great deal to help her not to be overprotective with her own children.

Overprotection by the mother, which E. A. Strecker terms "momism" or "smother love," is a real problem in present day American family life.[9]   The counselor must be on the alert for it in those who come for premarital counseling.   Unless the "psychological umbilical cord" is cut before marriage, it may be very difficult for a good marital relationship to develop.   A frank discussion and fearless evaluation of the parent-child relationship can do much to correct overprotectiveness.   An understanding of one's striving for independence as natural in the course of the development of the personality often comes as a sudden illumination of a parent-child situation which had resulted in resentment and guilt.

After a few months of marriage a young wife came to say she was ready to leave her husband.   He was an only child of wealthy parents who had never allowed him to think for himself.   He was totally inadequate in marriage.   He could make no decisions, depended upon his parents, who visited the young couple constantly and insisted on the couple's visiting them.   They continued to buy his clothes and now had begun to criticize the wife.

After I talked with the husband, what the wife said was confirmed.   He loved his wife and wanted to make a success of his marriage.   He wanted to understand himself and his parents.   After a number of conferences he began to make good progress in overcoming his inadequacies.   Hearing of the counseling, the parents, who had become concerned about the marriage, also came to talk with the counselor.   In this case, they took the initiative in cutting the apron strings and began to stay out of the affairs of the young couple with the result that the son began to mature and assume his responsibilities.

Strong marriages begin in the home during the formative years

[9] For a discussion of "Momism," see Edward A. Strecker, *Their Mothers' Sons: The Psychiatrist Examines an American Problem* (Philadelphia: J. B. Lippincott Company, 1951).

when the bases for healthy personalities are laid. Adequacy in meeting life's situations is one of the foundation stones in building a successful marriage.

Self-actualization

This is the goal to which every normal person aspires. It means to reach the full potential of one's capabilities. "What a man *can* be, he *must* be." (Maslow) As one's needs are satisfied, powerful latent energies are released and one is free to strive toward higher goals of achievement. The healthy personality is ever seeking to enhance itself. As fears, anxieties, and guilt are removed the personality seems to stretch and begin to reach out for long denied goals as a prisoner freed from his chains rejoices in his liberty.

For the Christian, self-actualization means to become all that God intends one to be in his moral integrity which includes, of course, his relationships with other people. This brings us again to the object of premarital counseling which is to enable two people to so live together that they will establish a small unit of the Kingdom of God into which will come children who will in turn be enabled to find their place in the Kingdom and extend its influence to others with whom they come in contact. The Christian home should be a place where every member, understanding his physiological needs and how they may be met, is enabled to move on to learning how his psychological needs may be met in an atmosphere that promotes mental health through wholesome interpersonal relationships based on the Christian concept of love. Self-actualization is difficult, if not impossible, to achieve in a "sick" marriage. Therefore, in all premarital counseling by the minister, let him keep in mind that he is seeking to help his couples form "healthy" marriages out of which will come strong, earnest Christians capable of demonstrating the Christian way of life. The Christian seeks self-realization through self-sacrifice. In no other relationship does one find such day to day primary self-sacrifice as in marriage. A healthy marriage naturally elicits this giving of the self for another through sacrifice.

Summary

In presenting this chapter on personality needs, it is not intended to imply that the minister-counselor must be a professional in the field of human behavior. But, in helping a couple understand their needs, and what they can do in meeting each other's needs, the minister can go far in relieving them of many anxieties and in helping them build a marriage in which their children will have their needs met so that they in turn may also build happy and successful marriages.

8

Difficult areas of adjustment

*L*et us turn now to the more specifically structured part of the personal interviews. Some
areas of difficult adjustment must be gone into, if at all possible.
This is one reason why couples should be encouraged to give ample
notice of at least three months of their approaching marriage to
the minister. As already mentioned, time is always a factor in premarital counseling. Only by carefully structuring the interviews
can these areas be covered within the time usually available.

I am indebted to Judson T. Landis for the chart (p. 143) of
areas of adjustment.

It is suggested that the order in which the areas of adjustment
are taken up be varied according to the interviewee and information obtained in the reconnaissance, taking up the most serious
problem of adjustment first. However, it is my experience that sex
adjustment is best taken up last, the reason being that most men
and women are not accustomed to discussing sex matters with the
minister, or with any professional person. They need to become

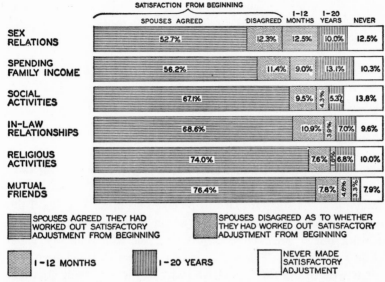

Percentage of 818 spouses reporting various periods of time required after marriage to achieve adjustment in six areas. People who had been successfully married for an average of 20 years had experienced greater difficulty in adjusting in certain areas. From Judson T. Landis, "Length of Time Required to Achieve Adjustment in Marriage," *American Sociological Review*, 11:6 (December, 1946), 668. Reprinted in Landis and Landis, *Building a Successful Marriage*, 3rd ed. (Prentice-Hall), p. 356.

better acquainted and to feel more at ease with the counselor before getting into the area of sexual adjustment. In view of the hush-hush way in which sex is treated in our American culture many people are embarrassed by their ignorance and also feel guilty about some of their sex thoughts and practices. Consequently, the atmosphere is much more tolerant to the discussion of sex matters when the subject is taken up last in the personal interviews. However, this must not be construed as indicating that it may be taken up if there is time, or that it can be treated lightly. The last interview should be left for this primarily, and if there is time for any other area.

The Presbyterian Church in the United States indicates these same areas of adjustment in its statement regarding premarital counseling:

Attention shall be given to all important aspects of marriage, especially those where problems may arise, whether they be physical, emotional, economic, social, moral or religious. (See Appendix III.)

Finances

Since the second area in which couples have their greatest difficulty in working out satisfactory adjustment is in spending the family income, I suggest that this be taken up first. Usually, if the person is asked to mention areas in which he has heard it is difficult to work out a satisfactory adjustment, he will generally name finances or money. This makes it very natural to begin here.

It is wise to ask the interviewee why this is a difficult area and let him explain in his own way. A question here and there will help him to explore the problem and come up with some very good solutions.

Also, asking how the problem was worked out in his own home may lead to some good objective thinking. After some evaluation has been made of his family's ways of handling finances, it is well to ask him to tell how he and his wife plan to handle theirs. This will lead into practical suggestions the counselor may wish to make.

I cannot go here into great detail on the economic aspects of family life. Many books have been written on this subject. They are very good and will be of real value to the counselor.[1] The seriousness of the problem is shown in the Landis' study[2] in which it was revealed that it had taken the 409 older couples (all had been married an average of 20 years or more) longer to work out problems centering around the spending of the family income than

[1] Landis & Landis, Building a Successful Marriage, Chaps. 19, 20, 21. Ray E. Baber, Marriage and the Family, Chap. 12.
[2] Landis & Landis, Building a Successful Marriage, p. 356.

problems in any other area except sex relations. Approximately one couple in five had never satisfactorily agreed on finances. My survey showed it to be the most difficult area of the six.

Some of the suggestions I make are as follows:

1. Let the wife be responsible for running the house and paying ordinary household bills: grocery, light, water, telephone, clothes for herself and children. This gives the wife training in handling money. Let the husband be responsible for paying the larger items such as rent, insurance, taxes, automobile payments, and business investments.

2. Let the husband give the wife an allowance ample for the budget they will have worked out together. Having given her the allowance, he should let her bank it and spend it as she thinks best. The wife's thriftiness will soon be felt, and if the husband compliments her on it, this will give her encouragement and self-confidence. Of course, as time goes on the allowance will have to be increased. Wives who are not allowed by their husbands to learn to handle family finances, may be unable to assume this responsibility in case of the husband's prolonged illness or death.

3. Often, a joint bank account is apt to lead to friction. It can be successfully used only if there is complete trust on both sides. Now it is good to have a joint checking account which the wife may use in emergencies, and I recommend that. For I have seen situations in which all the money was in the husband's name, and the wife was unable to get any for emergency needs due to the husband's injury, illness or death.

4. If the wife works, it is best that the combined incomes not be pooled and spent for current expenses. This gives a false impression of having a large income. Then when the wife becomes pregnant and must stop work, the income suddenly drops and the scale of living planned on their combined incomes comes to a sudden end. Of course, nowadays when many wives work to put their husbands through college, the use of their income must be planned according to the special nature of this arrangement. Otherwise, where the husband is working, my suggestion is that

the wife use her income for something of permanent value to the home, or deposit it so as to draw interest with the long-range plan of using it for a down payment on a lot or house or furniture— for something of lasting value.

It is very important that a husband feel and bear the responsibility for providing his family with the necessities: food, clothes, and shelter. When the wife pays for these things, it takes something away from the husband that is vital to his role. Of course, as already said, putting her husband through college is excepted. Yet, even here she is using her income for something of permanent value to the family.

5. Every family needs insurance and savings. Even if they can put aside only a very small amount each payday, they should do it. Some engaged couples start a joint savings account and continue it after marriage. The day will come when they will need some ready cash, and it gives a couple a sense of security to know that there is something in hand beside the pay check.

Every counselor will have his own suggestions for the spending of the family income. Going over the matter carefully with the couple individually helps them to be more objective about it and also enables them to discuss it between themselves before marriage.

Social and recreational activities

According to Landis' study, social activities was the third most difficult area of adjustment. In my survey it was sixth. This includes recreational activities. Often after marriage there is some tendency on the part of husband and wife for each to go his or her own way in reaching social and recreational outlets for divergence and companionship. Some of this is natural and must be recognized and accepted in marriage. Spouses who have normal social activities with their own sex will return to the husband-wife relationship with more alacrity than those who are "compelled" to seek these outlets only in company with the other spouse. On the other hand, it is also true that the more activities spouses enjoy together, the happier will be their marriage.

Mrs. X. came for counseling in great indignation, saying that ever since her marriage her husband had neglected her for a group of cronies who met at a small restaurant. But upon questioning it was apparent that she exaggerated. Very often they went out together—movies, dinner, ball games, and parties. He occasionally sought the outlet to which she objected. In her mind this over-shadowed all the activities they enjoyed together, for she was reacting to what she perceived to be the real situation: his neglect of her for his male companions. So long as she perceived it this way, it was real to her and she remained unhappy. A person reacts to a situation or an environment as it is experienced and perceived. "The perceptual field is, for the individual, 'reality'." [3] Although she had her own social outlets with her women friends such as clubs and church groups, she did not appreciate his need for male companionship. After this kind of situation has gone on for some time, the conflict is not quickly or easily resolved. That is why it is important to discuss the area of social activities and recreation before marriage so that each partner will recognize and appreciate the needs of the other for social and recreational outlets with his or her own sex.

Families are being encouraged more and more to do things together. A home, after all, is a cooperative enterprise. Each member of the family must have an interest in making his con-tribution to the development of the home. A wife alone cannot make a home; nor can a husband without the wife's help. To-gether, any mature couple can complement each other and from each one's heritage can bring the best of each and contribute it to the building of the home, so that, as the years pass, the home will be the sum-product of the ideals, dreams, and efforts of husband and wife. There are countless activities in family living that spouses can engage in together. All these should be explored by couples. In premarital counseling, much can be done to help them see these avenues leading toward a successful marriage.

It is interesting to list the varied social and recreational activities couples enjoy together as shown by my survey: picnics with other couples, swimming parties, golf, dancing, movies, fishing, hunting, camping, bridge and other games, sports—things which are literally as varied as life itself. Most people like to dress up occasionally and go out to lunch or dinner, or call on friends. Couples who live to themselves soon lose social contacts, and their interests become circumscribed within a very small area.

Ann was a very sociable person; she liked parties. She enjoyed having people in her home for tea or bridge, or just to spend an evening talking. Jim was bored with it all. He grumbled every time she took him out and became so rude that they were invited out less and less. In tears, she told how he had gone so far as to be rude to guests they were entertaining. She concluded, "Now we go nowhere and no one comes to see us."

A husband complained that his wife never wanted to go anywhere or do anything. "She just wants to stay home, and I'm tired of it." I am sure that much unhappiness of this sort can be prevented if this area of adjustment is gone into by the counselor before the marriage. Couples should learn to meet their social contacts together, and develop skills in hospitality.

It is encouraging to see wives learning to fish and hunt so that they may enjoy these recreational activities with their husbands; and it is equally encouraging to see husbands who welcome their wives into these activities. At the beach we may see whole families fishing and crabbing together. These experiences are wholesome and never to be forgotten.

To promote social and recreational activities within a marriage requires thought and planning, for like any other aspect of married life, good results do not just happen. They have to be earned, and this requires work. But it may mean the difference between success or failure of the marriage. It also points to the fact that for a couple to live together happily without tension, each must consider the social and recreational needs of the other.

In-law relationships

More attention is being paid today to in-laws and their influence upon marriage than ever before. In-laws can destroy the foundations for a good marriage carefully laid in premarital counseling. Every counselor has seen this happen. I feel that the significant in-law or in-laws on each side should be asked to come in for counseling before the marriage. This is not always possible because they may not live in the same town as the engaged couple. In some cases I have insisted on an interview with the in-laws; and in other cases I wish that I had done so, because soon after marriage in-law trouble began.

A well-to-do socially prominent city girl came for premarital counseling. She was engaged to the son of a small town mechanic who was poor and had little education. The son was a college graduate. The girl was concerned about how the two families would get along. They really had nothing in common. They had not met, though she had visited in the boy's home. I arranged for the parents to meet first at a "neutral place"—not in either home or town—so as to remove the obviously far apart background. The meeting and dinner went off fine. Subsequent meetings at the wedding and later were made much easier because of the careful plans made for the first meeting. A good relationship continues.

Very unpleasant in-law problems could have arisen. Also, the couple decided they would not live near either family. Premarital counseling helped them to work out the psychological problem of social distance and in-law relationships.

There is no need to conceal the fact that the mother-in-law causes more trouble than any other family figure in our culture. She is a notorious figure in the family life drama. She need not be so if she can be made to realize that the marriage of her son or daughter is a crisis in her life and that in order to meet the crisis she needs counseling.

In the premarital counseling this relationship must be dealt with specifically and thoroughly. Inquiry must be made into the existing relationship between the couple and in-laws on both sides. How close are the young people to their parents? If one, or both, is an only child, his or her relationship may be so close to one or both parents as to endanger the marriage from its beginning. Can they give up their parents? Can the parents give up their children?

I recall a couple whose daughter was 23 years of age and engaged to a fine young man. She was an adopted child and her parents objected very strenuously to her proposed marriage. They insisted that she was too immature to assume the responsibilities of homemaking. Actually, she was quite mature, earned her own living, and was a very capable young woman. Encouraged by the counselor to cut the "psychological umbilical cord" and make her own decision about her marriage, she told the parents gently but firmly what she intended to do. To her surprise, they accepted it. The marriage went off with their cooperation and with no interference from them afterward.

If one comes from a one-child family, the mother or the father may be very jealous of the man or woman who in marriage is "taking my daughter or son from me" as the mother-in-law may express it. This is true in one sense, but not in the sense that the mother or father sees it subjectively. That is the way in which they act, and will proceed to get back the child even to destroying the marriage if necessary. One mother-in-law, during the husband's absence, moved her only child out of his house and took her home. She never returned. No other factual cause could account for the divorce which followed later.

Sometimes, circumstances come about which demand that one of the in-laws live with the couple. This can be very serious, especially if the in-law is a domineering person, or if it is a mother-in-law who comes in to take over the house. If it is the husband's mother she may become very critical of the wife, criticizing her housekeeping, cooking, and social activities; if it is the wife's mother, she may criticize the husband for lack of attention, rudeness, laziness, or niggardliness.

A man came for counseling saying that when he got home for lunch he found a note from his wife informing him that she had left and would return only when he had gotten "rid of that woman," meaning his mother who had moved in three years before and taken over. The husband said that he had "gone through hell" between them. Now his wife was gone. What should he do? He concluded that he would put his home first, take his mother to a relative, and bring his wife back. This he did, almost within the hour! His mother protested violently, accusing him of lack of filial love and respect. But the man stuck by his decision. Since that time several years have passed. At last report their home was a happy and peaceful one. The mother, who had another son and daughter, also found new interests by living part of the year with each, including the son who had the unpleasant duty of taking his mother to his sister, saying, "It is your turn now to have mother."

An important principle: our home first. There is one principle every couple should be made to face in regard to in-law relationships, and that is "our home must come first." After all, is not that what Jesus meant when He said, "For this reason a man shall leave his father and mother and be joined to his wife, and the two shall become one"? [4] When a couple start their marriage on this principle, in-law relationships can be worked out.

Several practical solutions may be suggested. Mr. and Mrs. Y. had been married several years and had three children when financial reasons made it necessary for her mother to live with them. Things went fairly well for a year or so when Mr. Y. began to complain about various little things concerning his mother-in-law. His wife noticed that he would "sulk" in the evening over very trivial things. Finally, one night when he returned home he became quarrelsome with his mother-in-law and the children. Later

[4] Mark 10:7.

in the evening, when he and his wife were alone, he issued his ultimatum: "Either your mother goes, or I go. We are never alone with each other or the children. Always she is present— morning, noon and night. I'm sick of the sight of her."

The wife was able to see that regardless of her mother, her home had to come first, and, with that as a frame of reference, some practical solution could be worked out. In the end she decided to tell her mother that thereafter she would have her breakfast and supper in her room. They would have lunch together since the husband did not come home for lunch. She would spend her evenings in her room unless asked to come into the living room with the family. Her mother protested her daughter did not love her, but having no choice, acquiesced reluctantly in the plan. The family atmosphere cleared at once. About a month later, Mr. Y. suggested inviting "the old lady," as he called her, "to supper." After that he frequently wanted her to join them for supper, or Sunday dinner, or come in for the evening. A few months later he told me how well things were going, and added, "You know, I like that old lady now."

Other couples have worked out other solutions: a near-by apartment for the in-laws, an addition to the house such as a bedroom, bath and kitchenette for the husband's parents, or a garage apartment for the old couple. Mature planning together can solve in-law problems of this nature. Some young couples run unexpectedly into this problem soon after marriage. Some find conditions such that they feel they must live with parents on one side or the other. This should be avoided if at all possible. One couple faced with this probability, in spite of protests, and at great sacrifice, moved into a low rent apartment. Perhaps all young couples would do well to start off together in some other town apart from all in-laws. This has happened for many army couples. Although no statistics are available, it is my impression that many of these couples who had their first year or two together far enough away to avoid in-law interference, made better adjustment with each other than they might have done had they lived with or near in-laws.

Religious activities

Landis' study shows religious activities to fall into fifth place in time required after marriage to achieve a satisfactory adjustment. In my study of couples who had received premarital counseling this area fell in third place—that is, the third most difficult area of adjustment. This may be explained by the fact that Landis' couples were chosen without regard to religion, whereas the couples I studied had all been married in the Church, and at least one spouse was an Episcopalian—usually the woman, because marriages usually take place in the bride's church. Among the Episcopal couples, 70 per cent made a satisfactory adjustment in religion during the first year. However, in the control group[5] only 56.3 per cent of Episcopal couples reported a satisfactory adjustment the first year.

Religion should be a unifying force in the home, and couples who belong to the same church and participate in the life of the church seem to work out many difficulties which might lead other couples to divorce. This does not mean necessarily that church couples are happy in their marriage, for some very unhappy couples remain married because they do not believe in divorce. However, we might safely conclude that religious influence is a factor in stabilizing a marriage and increasing marital happiness. Landis reports:

Research studies show that in general, in our culture, the presence of a religious faith is associated with more favorable chances for marital success. . . . Our study of 409 couples showed regular church attendance to be among the factors associated with happiness in marriage. . . .

When the measure is marital permanence or marital break-up, studies

[5] Composed of 186 white couples married in Episcopal churches of a large southern city.

covering approximately 25,000 marriages have shown that there were three times as many marital failures among people with no religious affiliation as among those within given religions. In marriages between persons of different religions, religion may be a disruptive factor, yet the failure rate of marriages of mixed religions is generally lower than that of marriages where there is no religion.[6]

A study made by Burgess and Cottrell revealed that those who participated regularly in religious activities, such as attendance at Church and Sunday School, made a better adjustment in marriage than those who never attended or stopped attending before they were 18 years of age.[7]

Terman, reporting on the results of his study on happy and unhappy men, says

Unfavorable attitudes toward religious work and interests characterize more of the unhappy men.   A larger percentage of the unhappy believe that religions do more harm than good, dislike Bible study, and dislike work with Y.M.C.A. or K.C.   Happy men, on the contrary, are a distinct majority among those who like Bible study, dislike irreligious people, or believe it essential that children should have religious instruction.[8]

Very strict religious training is as detrimental to one's interest in religion as little or no religious training.   Terman suggests that either very much or very little religious training may be less favorable to marital happiness than a more moderate amount.

James A. Peterson, in a study relating high and low adjustment of married men and women to religious types, found that those belonging to liberal religious groups have the highest level of adjustment while those belonging to institutional—authoritarian groups have the lowest level of adjustment.[9]

[6] Landis & Landis, *Building a Successful Marriage*, pp. 429-431.
[7] E. W. Burgess and L. S. Cottrell, Jr., *Predicting Success or Failure in Marriage* (Englewood Cliffs, N. J.: Prentice-Hall, Inc., 1939), p. 12.
[8] Lewis Terman, *Psychological Factors in Marital Happiness*, (New York: McGraw-Hill Book Company, Inc., 1939), p. 164.
[9] James A. Peterson, *Education for Marriage* (New York: Charles Scribner's Sons, 1956), pp. 327-328.

In his discussion of divorced and happily married couples, Locke stated that a church wedding, church membership, church attendance, and active participation in Sunday School before and during marriage resulted in a larger percentage of happily married couples. A person who is a church member is usually thought to be conventional and sociable. Such attitudes contribute to good marital adjustment.[10]

The minister-counselor should be very careful not to try to persuade either partner to affiliate with the minister's church. It is my policy to suggest: (1) that they be in the same church; (2) that if the man is interested and active in his church, the woman should join his church; (3) but, if not, and if the woman is interested and active in her church, the man should become a member of her church; (4) and if neither can accept the other's church, that they seek a third church in which both may worship and work together.

Many ministers will not agree with this position, but I feel very strongly that religion should unify a marriage, and it can best do this if both spouses are together in the same church. Since responsibility for religion in the home should rest upon the husband, his position in that regard is strengthened if the couple accepts his church, provided, of course, that it is of primary importance to him. Sometimes a woman will leave her church to go into her husband's, hoping this may get him interested in his church. Too often, it results in neither of them participating in any church. Premarital counseling gives the minister an unusual opportunity to discuss religion and the Church with the bride and groom in a constructive way, leading both of them to a decision about the Church which will start them off anticipating a good church relationship during the years ahead.

In premarital counseling I emphasize religion as a unifying force in the home. Couples are encouraged to use religion creatively and to maintain a close relationship to the Church.

[10] Harvey J. Locke, *Predicting Adjustment in Marriage* (New York: Henry Holt and Company, 1951), pp. 239-241.

Mutual friends

Making a satisfactory adjustment in mutual friends relationship is the least difficult area in Landis' study, and is next to the least difficult among the couples and the least difficult among individuals in my study.

If couples marry in their own social group, their friends are apt to be of that group; consequently, no particular problems will arise. If the man and woman come from different social levels, their friends can become real problems in making a happy marriage.

Jane complained violently about her husband's ill-mannered friends who came to the house; but he complained just as bitterly about her snobbish bridge-playing friends. During the war, girls married soldiers about whose home and background they knew nothing. Many were disillusioned when the war was over and they went to their husband's town and met his family and friends. This also happens where they come from distant towns and are unacquainted with the social life of each other's community. It is always wise for them to visit each other's family and to meet some of their friends before marriage.

After marriage, couples usually make friends together among married acquaintances. Choosing friends together, they are more apt to choose those with whom both are congenial.

It is interesting to note that in my study an early adjustment in social activities and in mutual friends showed a high positive correlation with membership in the same church. During the first year of marriage 82.8 per cent of the experimental group and 93.7 per cent of the control group made a satisfactory adjustment in their social activities. Likewise, during the first year of marriage 92.9 per cent of the experimental group and 95.8 per cent of the control group made a satisfactory adjustment in their mutual friends relationships. This is what should have been expected since couples naturally find some of their social activities and friends within the membership of the same church, which is further reason for strongly urging a couple to be in the same church.

Sex relations

Landis found this to be the most difficult area of adjustment. I found that it was the third most difficult area in the control group, and fourth most difficult area in the experimental group. The respective positions were based upon an early adjustment, indicating that the premarital counseling on sex relations received by the experimental group brought about less difficult adjustment in sex relations than that experienced by Landis' group and the control group couples who had little or no counseling on sex. It must be pointed out that some in the control group said that they had discussed sex relations with their doctor which no doubt accounts for this area being third place.

Although sex is not the most important part of married life, its place within the marriage relationship must not be minimized. Happiness and success in marriage are directly related to satisfactory sex adjustment. In my study it was found that an early adjustment in sex relations was definitely related to marital happiness. Landis' study showed the same result. In commenting on his findings Landis says:

Sex relationships, more often than some other phases of marital interaction, seem to be the focal point of tensions, because constantly recurring biological urges force couples to reckon with this part of life. Two people who differ on religion may possibly agree to disagree and live together happily; a couple may have widely divergent ideas concerning the use of money, yet if they have enough money so that their differences do not cause financial hardship, they can tolerate their differences and live in peace. But in the area of sex the issue must be faced; for the sex urge is comparable to hunger in that it seeks periodic satisfaction. It also requires cooperation. Differences here cannot be ignored as can some other differences. Therefore, although sex is not an all-important factor in itself, a mutually gratifying sex relationship will serve to facilitate all adjustments, just as conflicts seemingly unrelated to sex will have repercussions in the sex life of the couple.

Although the place of sex in marriage is too often exaggerated, the contribution it makes to successful marriage is nevertheless important. Certainly few marriages would take place were it not for sexual attraction between the two partners; so throughout life the sex attraction can serve to enhance and to color all the couple's association together. Studies among happily married couples all agree that couples who have achieved the highest degree of mutuality in their sex relations are among the most happily married.

The personality traits that each partner takes into marriage will have much to do with the degree of sexual mutuality achieved. People who are cooperative, perceptive of the reactions of others, and considerate of the needs of others are the ones who seek to share gratification rather than having as their goal self-gratification only. Those who are selfish, impatient, unaware of the needs of others, and unwilling to learn from others will have far less to contribute toward the achievement of a rewarding sex relationship in marriage. These personality factors are of far greater importance in sex adjustment than simple biological adequacy is.[11]

With all the importance placed upon sex in marriage, there are enduring marriages in which because of accident or illness the sex act has been eliminated. A fine illustration is that of a wife who was hospitalized for many years during which time coitus was not possible. Her husband, remaining faithful to her, was outstanding in his devotion. He was kind and considerate. His weekends were spent in long visits with her. In spite of her affliction and considerable suffering, she was remarkably bright and cheerful reflecting her sense of being loved by her husband. There is far more to marriage than sex, and those who marry for sex are emotionally immature. Their love is on the eros level.

However, since sex adjustment is so important to a happy mar-

[11] Landis & Landis, *Building a Successful Marriage*, pp. 378-379.

riage, the next chapter will deal with this subject as it relates to the personal interviews.

Summary

Since all of the six areas of adjustment are in the future for individuals being counseled, marriage problems which may arise in these areas can be dealt with only in generalities. While there is no substitute for scientific knowledge in any of the six areas, there are other factors which affect the adjustment for good or bad. Burgess and Cottrell summarized by saying:

> In short, the outstanding factors in marital adjustment seem to be those of affection, temperamental compatibility, and social adaptability. The biological and economic factors are of less importance and appear to be largely determined by these other factors.[12]

This causes one to conclude that the effectiveness of premarital counseling lies more in helping individuals to a better understanding of themselves and their individual personality problems than in merely disseminating knowledge in the six areas, though this, too, is important.

[12] Burgess and Cottrell, *Predicting Success or Failure in Marriage*, p. 349.

9

Sex instruction for marriage

As pointed out in Chapter 8 sex intruction for marriage should be taken up last in the personal interviews. Many individuals are quite reticent about discussing sex. But if the pastor has established through the previous interviews a good relationship, based upon confidence in his ability to help the couple toward a happy and successful marriage, then he should have little difficulty in discussing sex with them individually.

Use of the Sex Knowledge Inventory

I have found the use of the Sex Knowledge Inventory, Form X, very helpful.[1]

[1] This inventory has been developed by Gelolo McHugh, Ph.D., and may be obtained from Family Life Publications, Inc., 6725 College Station, Durham, N.C.

Sex Knowledge Inventory, Form Y may be obtained from the same address. This test measures individual understanding of the human reproductive system, knowledge of how sex organs function, and vocabulary pertaining to sexual activity. Form Y can be used independently or to supplement Form X. Form X objectively measures sex knowledge through 80 multiple choice questions, one of which is to be checked as the correct one. It is accompanied by a Marriage Counselor's Manual which explains the purpose of each question and the correct answer. A scoring sheet and manual accompany the forms. There is a question blank for each individual. It usually requires 40 minutes to an hour to complete the inventory. Directions are complete on each set of questions.

The Sex Knowledge Inventory provides discussional openings to cover more items of sex knowledge and attitudes than would be likely to come up in even two or more interviews without them. They locate quickly key areas of misinformation and indicate unhealthy feelings concerning sex which so often are relevant to personal problems discussed in counseling. Most important of all, the test makes a major therapeutic contribution to premarital counseling, because it gives evidence to the counselee that what he knows, or does not know, is not unique to himself and that a lack of sex knowledge is neither unusual, bad, nor peculiar. This modifies self-concern about sex and tends to de-emotionalize sex from fear-provoking attitudes and beliefs to a matter of fact consideration.

A date should be set for the individuals to come in to take the test a few days prior to the time for this interview. They should be asked not to discuss with each other the inventory until both have completed it.

Use of the inventory prepares the way for the discussion of sex with the pastor by removing some of the inhibition the couple may have. It also seems to increase the confidence of the couple in the counselor.

Present day attitude toward sex

Although the attitude toward sex is gradually changing, there are still large segments of our population whose attitude is Victorian and puritanical. Many young parents are eager to adopt new and wholesome attitudes but still struggle against the impressions of childhood that sex is vile, dirty, or even evil. A young woman preparing for marriage, who kept putting off the date with one excuse then another, was actually afraid of the sex relationship because of the ugly things her mother had said to her about it.

Some still come to marriage with the idea that sex is only to be enjoyed by the husband; the wife must endure it. Others have been told that masturbation will bring impotence, or, more generally, insanity. And there are those who believe that intercourse weakens one physically. There are many such taboos connected with sex and it would be impossible to take them all up here. It is not the purpose of the interview to dwell on the taboos but to encourage a wholesome attitude toward sex. Some individuals will have been deeply impressed with some one or two taboos which may be ascertained as the Sex Knowledge Inventory is discussed. These should be explained.

Traumatic sex experiences

Some individuals, especially girls, have received traumatic sex experiences when young which should be brought out and faced objectively in the light of their present maturity. Among these experiences may be mentioned exposure, molesting, fondling, attempts at rape, seduction, or incest. These experiences may carry a very heavy guilt load coloring one's whole attitude toward sex.

For example, a man at 35 had not resolved his guilt feelings about an attempted intercourse with his sister when he was 8 years of age and she 6. Because of shame and guilt many people have never discussed their early sex experiences with anyone in a position to listen without condemning. It gives them great relief to ventilate these experiences in the presence of a trusted counselor. The pastor must not probe. The following question might be sufficient: "Have you had any frightening sex experiences in childhood or since, that you would like to discuss?" To attempt to coerce one into revealing things he does not wish to share with the pastor, may alienate the counselee and the pastor permanently.

Sexual freedom

Many sex taboos and considerable "hush-hush" still surround the subject of sex today. These blocks must be removed if wholesome attitudes are to be built in our young people.

I do not, of course, advocate sexual license. The point is that many persons who come for counseling will have had disturbing experiences which may have been frightening, disgusting or left them feeling ashamed and guilty. Some of these experiences may have involved the person one plans to marry. For there is considerable freedom today among young people in their discussion of sex and familiarity between boys and girls. It is not uncommon for engaged couples to have intercourse, or to have engaged in "heavy petting" resulting in orgasm. Some couples will have such a sense of guilt that they will feel they must marry in order to right the wrong—always a shaky foundation on which to build a marriage. Although the counselor should not condone what they have done, if the couple really loves each other and planned on marriage before intercourse took place, then it may be said that their union has been consummated already and the service of Holy Matrimony will be God's blessing upon it.

The minister-counselor can do much to help such couples in their effort to resist further sexual intimacies until marriage, for they may want very sincerely to conform to Christian ethics, realizing that such intimacies belong rightly to marriage and that coitus adds to marriage a uniqueness which distinguishes it from all other relationships. Although it is not the purpose of this manual to guide the minister in his pastoral work of ministering to such couples, by his patience, understanding, and love for a couple, he can, in his own way and according to his church's teaching and discipline, help the couple to receive God's forgiveness, forgive each other and find self-acceptance as "new creatures" in Christ Jesus. Some couples may wish to go into the church with the minister and make a formal confession in their own words, or say together a confession,[2] before God and him, after which the minister may read the absolution, or say a prayer, and pronounce a benediction according to his church's practice. Such couples should understand from all the counseling involved which leads up to confession and absolution that further sexual intimacy should be deferred until marriage.

The pastor who goes through this sort of counseling experience without being shocked or condemnatory will help the couple to accept their premarital sexual intimacies, although premature, as a part of the totality of their love and marital relationship.

It is more common than not for engaged couples to discuss quite freely the whole gamut of sex in marriage. They also read and discuss books on sex. Among the books loaned to a couple preparing for marriage should be included one or two good books on sex knowledge. (See Bibliography.) These books will enable a couple to discuss sex more freely with the pastor as the books will indicate to the couple that he has read the books and is prepared to discuss the subject objectively.

The minister's attitude in discussing sex

It is very essential that the counselor feel comfortable in discussing sex with an individual or couple. A great deal of harm can be done if he is nervous, ill-at-ease, and unsure of himself. His embarrassment will increase the emotionality of the counseling session and deepen any fears and apprehension on the part of the counselee who may be very hesitant and fearful anyway.

[2] *Book of Common Prayers*, pp. 6 and 75.

The minister's position

Before attempting to counsel with a couple on sex matters the minister should examine his own position in three respects:

Factual sex knowledge. Factual sex knowledge will do much to discharge some of his emotional feelings by helping him to be objective. The anatomy of the genital region should be familiar to him. Charts which may be found in various books should be memorized and the function of each organ well understood. Several books are recommended for him to read. One book, *The Wonder of Life,* by Milton Levine, M.D. and Jean H. Seligmann is particularly good. (See Bibliography for publishers of recommended books.) This book is written for boys and girls entering adolescence. One may wonder why it is recommended for adults. I have found in lending the book to parents for their children's reading, that the parents invariably express appreciation for its help to them. This may be because it takes one back to one's own adolescence in the language of that age and psychologically removes some of the fears many had in those years. Also, in connection with this book, and in developing in the Church a sex education program, there are a number of short films available. One I have used successfully with confirmation classes and parents groups is *Human Growth.* Other books for the pastor and couples are *Sex Without Fear* by Lewin and Gilmore; *Modern Pattern for Marriage* by Walter R. Stokes; *A Doctor's Marital Guide for Patients* by Bernard R. Greenblat; and *Whom God Hath Joined* by David R. Mace, a very helpful book of daily readings covering the purpose of Christian marriage, its objects, and standards.

Having in one's mind factual knowledge of sex does not necessarily mean that one can discuss the matter objectively and unemotionally. This comes only by actual experiences in discussing it. Therefore, it is suggested that the minister go over these matters with his wife or a male friend, perhaps another minister. Let each explain the charts to the other until the anatomy and function of the genital region is clear to both.

Another suggestion is that the pastor complete the Sex Knowledge Inventory himself, score it and go over each item with the manual. Two pastors might do this together; that is, each complete the inventory and, using the manual, discuss their answers.

An objective attitude. Although factual sex knowledge will help one toward a wholesome attitude toward sex, that alone will not overcome one's early impressions, teaching and guilt feelings about sex. These matters should also be discussed freely, preferably with a trusted male friend. Whether these matters, which may be highly emotionally charged, can be discussed with one's wife, will depend upon the wife's understanding of psychology and her flexibility in accepting hitherto unrevealed experiences of her husband. For one to discuss with a male friend problems of masturbation, sex curiosity, and experiences, frustrations, fears and guilt, will enable him to gain objectivity and a wholesome attitude so that he will feel at ease when others discuss these matters with him.

Sex: good, not evil. The counselor must be convinced, himself, that sex is good: that there is no evil in sex itself; but that the evil we associate with it and the manner in which we have corrupted it has come, as Jesus said, "out of the heart of man." David R. Mace writes:

> One of the powerful forces that draw men and women together in marriage is the drive of sexual desire. This is a normal, healthy, God-given impulse. It is also a strong and insistent urge. It has to be so; otherwise the vitally important function of reproduction might be neglected, and the continuing purpose of creation would be defeated.[3]

God gave us sex desire: (1) to reproduce the race; (2) to enrich our lives in marriage by means of the most intimate sharing of the self in a spiritual union with the object of one's love and in

[3] From *Whom God Hath Joined* by David R. Mace. Copyright, 1953, by W. L. Jenkins, The Westminster Press. Used by permission. P. 22.

which union each derives an indescribable pleasure; (3) to enhance man's life by sharing in the development of the sciences and the humanities. The pastor who has a wholesome attitude toward sex will convey the same to the individuals he counsels; indeed, to all of his people.

We have found it reassuring to individuals to read to them the pronouncements their church has made on sex in marriage. If a pastor finds that his church has not yet issued any statement on the subject, he should read what other churches have said.

The Lambeth Conference of 1958 officially declared:

It has long been held that a primary obligation of Christian marriage is that children may be born within the supporting framework of parental love and family concern, with a right to an opportunity for a full and spiritually wholesome life. Yet we believe that the procreation of children is not the sole purpose of Christian marriage. Implicit within the bond between husband and wife is the relationship of love with its sacramental expression in physical union. Because these two great purposes of Christian marriage illumine each other and form the focal points of constructive home life, we believe that family planning, in such ways as are mutually acceptable to husband and wife in Christian conscience, and secure from the corruptions of sensuality and selfishness, is a right and important factor in Christian family life. (See Appendix I.)

Morbid curiosity to be avoided

Since sex is one of the most fascinating subjects for discussion, the counselor must be very careful not to be carried away by curiosity regarding the knowledge and experiences counselees may bring up. Unless he is trained in psychology and is a skilled psychotherapist, the counselor should be content with the counselee's relating of simple facts, receiving them without any show of surprise or emotional shock.

Discussing the Sex Knowledge Inventory

By the time this interview is held, a warm, friendly and trustful feeling toward the counselor will have been generated in the individual, making it easy to take up the subject of sex in marriage.

By way of introduction, I have found it helpful to explain the success and failure in sex adjustment as noted on the chart in Chapter 8. (See p. 143.) The question naturally arises: Why should sexual adjustment in marriage be so difficult since, because of its naturalness, one would expect it to be the least difficult area of adjustment?

When we seek the answer to this problem, two observations generally are made: (1) lack of sex knowledge; (2) an unwholesome attitude toward sex.

It is then easy to move into the area of sex knowledge by explaining the diagrams of the male and female genital regions as found in the books recommended. If the counselee has read the books, then he may be well versed in this area; but he probably has never talked about it objectively with anyone in an unemotional atmosphere.

Woven into this explanation of the diagrams will be an orientation toward building a wholesome attitude.

The Sex Knowledge Inventory should then be taken up. Some of the items will have been covered in studying the diagrams. As time permits, the items should be gone over, question by question. However, if time does not permit, then the items missed and those circled should be taken up.

The minister's reassuring word

As the minister and counselee discuss the Christian attitude toward sex in marriage, its wholesomeness, its creativity, its culmination of the love relationship, one may witness a relaxation and acceptance on the part of the counselee. It is helpful to point out that "God created man in his own image, in the image of God he created him; male and female he created them. And God blessed them, and God said to them, 'Be fruitful and multiply' . . ." [4] Therefore, sex in marriage must be good and wholesome, for God would not create us to do evil. The sex act in marriage is acceptable and holy before God.

Intercourse between two people who love one another should produce not merely pleasure and satisfaction, but confidence, harmony, and self-respect. It should relieve anxiety, lessen guilt, and prevent the formation of hostility. All these consequences, being felt as a gift from the other partner, should fortify affection. To be indifferent to the physical expression of love, still more to dislike it, or to feel that it is in some way shameful, is neither superior nor virtuous nor refined; it is a symptom of mental illness or maladjustment.[5]

Wrong impressions corrected

If the counselee has been taught by parents that sex is evil or dirty, the word of the minister (who is a father figure) tends to correct the early impressions, and now the counselee seems to hear the parents say to him that sex in marriage is good and right. When any person has a self-reaction which carries a meaning of shame or doubt, only in the presence of some highly respected person as a father figure does the critical nature of the person's own self become lessened. He can now engage in sex relations with full parental approval. I do not mean to imply that this approbation of the pastor is alone sufficient to wipe out past impressions; but if the couple has been prepared by reading, adequate sex knowledge and discussion of attitudes, then the counselor's word may be the one reinforcement needed to help the couple begin their marriage with satisfactory sexual adjustment.

Lovemaking or sex play before intercourse should also be stressed

[4] Genesis 1:27, 28.
[5] Amber Blanco White, *Worry in Women* (London: Victor Gollancz, Ltd., 1941), pp. 162-163.

as a natural preliminary to the sex act. It should manifest kindness, consideration and respect for the feelings of each partner. Whatever is mutually agreeable may be done; but certainly nothing should be done that is non-acceptable to either. The mysterious sharing of their bodies, by which they become one flesh, is the highest expression of a couple's love and can be a deeply spiritual experience.

Preparation for marriage begun at birth

I never like to leave this interview without pointing out that couples can help their children gain a wholesome sex attitude so that they may not be ignorant of sex knowledge and develop an unwholesome attitude toward sex. Sex stimulation takes place in the baby in many ways: diaper changing, bathing, friction on the genitalia. The baby makes no emotional response to this stimulation. But the baby will be quick to discern in the parents any feelings of embarrassment or fear over this stimulation. Parents must be prepared for their children's sexual experiences of handling and playing with their sex organs. All of this should be accepted as natural and harmless. Masturbation should be overlooked.

Sex knowledge should be given the child as he asks questions and develops. When the child is old enough to look at pictures and be read to, I suggest among his other storybooks one entitled *Growing Up* by K. de Schweinitz, or some similar illustrated book. (See Bibliography.) There are many aids to parents in giving their children a sound sex education. When the mother is pregnant with the second child, this offers a fine opportunity to tell the first child what is taking place and in time to feel the movement of the fetus. Little children have no emotional feelings about sex, reproduction, pregnancy, or birth. They will accept the facts of life just as they accept facts about food, digestion, and elimination.

Of course, children should be taught the names of their sex organs just as they are taught (or should be) correct words for digestion and elimination. God made the whole body; therefore, all of it is good and beautiful to Him, and should be to us. If children are not told the names of their sex organs, they will assume that those parts of the body are not to be talked about except with other children in the language of the child's world. Likewise, they will seek answers to their questions about those parts of their body from other children or undesirable adults who purvey false and vulgar information. There is no substitute for sound, factual knowledge if a child is to develop a wholesome attitude toward sex.

Summary

Modern America is very sex conscious. Young people discuss sex quite freely. It is emphasized in novels and movies. Therefore, the minister-counselor must feel comfortable as he discusses sex in marriage with individuals. He must have factual sex knowledge and cultivate a wholesome and objective attitude toward sex.

The Sex Knowledge Inventory can be very helpful to the minister as well as to the individuals whom he counsels. Because of the minister's position, his word that sex is good can be reassuring to a couple as they anticipate coitus in marriage. He also has opportunity through sex instruction to correct many false ideas and wrong impressions of sex. He should seek to convey to the couple their responsibility in transmitting to their children a wholesome attitude toward sex.

V

THE OVERVIEW

10

The minister faces a new challenge

The minister who has given a couple his best in premarital counseling will have the satisfaction of a job well done. He will have guided the couple to the threshold of one of life's greatest crises. Together they will have discussed some of the couple's deepest emotional problems and shared their dreams of the future. The minister will have had the rare experience of walking on the lovers' own hallowed ground. Let him beware lest he clumsily bruise any of the flowers along the path! Let him beware lest he should ever betray their confidence!

The minister's capabilities

Time and again after discussing premarital counseling with minister groups, I am faced with the question of their ability to do premarital counseling as outlined in the previous chapters. "We are not psychologists," they say; or "We lack training in this field." My answer is that premarital counseling is such an important part of the minister's work that he must prepare himself to do it, either through private study, extension courses, or enrollment in the necessary courses in some university. In this regard Paul E. Johnson points out:

He (the minister) may feel unprepared to deal with such dynamic emotional factors. We do not say it will be easy or simple to deal with them, and yet we must learn and prepare to work with unconscious dynamics if we are to minister to the deepest needs of life. All of our relations are affected by these dynamic forces, and marriage will not escape them. Two whole persons are to know and seek to have each other in marriage, and if the pastor is to counsel them effectively he will enter into the depths of their emotional searching with them. If this is his responsibility he will want to have psychological training and competence to do so.

For we know that unconscious motives may defeat love, and wreck marriage by false expectations unwisely sought and often inimical to growing maturity. When marriage is entered into with illusive hopes and secret demands the course of such love is bound for distress and disappointment. To move from this mirage of illusion to realistic understanding and reasonable expectation is the goal of premarital counseling.[1]

The Methodist Church emphasizes the importance of the minister being trained in this field:

The time has come when every person planning marriage should have the opportunity for skilled and careful counseling by ministers or staff workers who are prepared in this field. If this is to be done, pastors must be trained to guide young people through premarital and post-marital counseling. [See Appendix II.]

The United Lutheran Church in America also advocates:

The church should provide opportunities for its pastors and lay leaders to prepare themselves to meet their responsibilities in ministering to

[1] Paul E. Johnson, "Emotional Problems in Premarital Counseling," *Pastoral Psychology*, December 1959, pp. 20-21.

families, and to young people contemplating marriage. This involves seminary training, in-service training opportunities, college courses, and special courses and institutes for lay leaders. Study material based on the view of marriage set forth in these summary statements should be provided. [See Appendix IV.]

On the scale presented in this book, premarital counseling is a new field of service for the pastor, but one which will bring to him such rewards that he will never regret the time or money spent in preparing for it. It will enrich his preaching, general counseling, and all his other pastoral functions.

Psychology as common knowledge

Much of the psychology presented in this book is common knowledge, recognizable as a part of the average minister's experience. One does not need a degree in psychology to understand and discuss the needs we all have for love and affection, or to be released from the bonds of guilt and fear. Ministers have always been getting these ideas across to their people as integral parts of the Gospel. They are woven in the very fabric of our Christian faith. Modern psychology helps us to understand the dynamics of these elements in the redemptive process—not only as they relate to God, but as husbands and wives relate to each other in marriage. Being on speaking terms with the current theories of the dynamics of personality and of personality structure enables the minister to understand his people and their behavior patterns, as well as his own. Often, just to be able to label one's feelings helps one to identify them so that he may deal with them in an objective and constructive manner. So if the minister is to serve his people skillfully and enable them to develop their personalities toward maturity in the Christian meaning, that is, developing "to mature manhood, to the measure of the stature of the fullness of Christ," [2] then it is encumbent upon the minister to be informed in the field of modern psychology.

[2] Ephesians 4:13.

Knowing the difficult areas of adjustment helps

As already pointed out, if a couple knows before the marriage the common areas of difficult adjustment required in marriage, much can be done in premarital counseling to help them deal successfully with the problems that may arise, or better, to help them prevent problems arising in those areas. If problems do arise they will be better prepared to resolve them. There are several books available dealing with these areas of adjustment which are recommended for a minister's library. (See Bibliography.) Again, I wish to stress that the personality factors are the main ones to be considered in premarital counseling rather than merely a study of the areas of adjustment; knowing how to keep within a budget will not solve a basic personality problem of resentment toward one's mother, which, without discrimination, may be transferred to one's wife.

The minister's opportunity

Premarital counseling gives the minister an opportunity that no other relationship with his people offers, to do basically constructive work in laying the foundations for strong Christian character in the next generation. Premarital counseling is preventive therapy for the family in the making. It is the best way to help the young couple plan intelligently and cooperatively for a happy and successful marriage out of which will come well-adjusted, happy children capable of living out their Christian faith.

Some resist premarital counseling

Some individuals will resist premarital counseling. There will be those who say, "Adults should be able to work out any problems which may arise in marriage"; or, "I have read books on sex so I know all I need to know about marriage"; or, "We have already discussed and agreed on everything." The minister must be patient with such people. He must show respect for their feelings and opinions. Explaining to them the purpose of premarital counseling as an aid to making the kind of marriage they want may help them to understand the minister's part in the counseling process and his motives in it. Even so, I have had a few individuals (not both parties) who resisted premarital counseling, and even refused it altogether, saying, "I can take care of any problem which may arise." There is no way by which the minister can force one into counseling. If there were, the counseling would probably be of little value. In my experience, in every case, one of the partners has always been receptive to the counseling.

Importance of teaching young people to expect premarital counseling

Teaching young people in the Church to expect premarital counseling will help greatly in their acceptance of it when the time comes. For we have one great yearning to count on: every normal person wants a happy marriage. Through premarital counseling the Church comes forward with a concrete and constructive program for her young couples and older ones, too.

Preparation for marriage should not wait until young people come for marriage. A number of churches are giving special attention to long-range preparation and are providing courses of instruction for young people on the Christian ideals of love, courtship and marriage. Many books, pamphlets and films are being produced to aid ministers in planning study groups on marriage, including courses on home building, income budgeting, child training, life adjustments, and personality problems.

The altar, the threshold of Christian marriage

When the couple stands before the altar to repeat their sacred vows, the minister stands with them to give them the Church's blessing in the name of God. The three together have blazed a trail through a wilderness of many problems and looked objectively upon the wreckage of many homes. They have come out to gaze upon a broad and fertile valley stretching toward the rough mountains of the unknown future. The road they are about to take leads through life's many adversities: threats to security, sickness, accidents, tragedies, for all these are a part of life and the testing ground of every marriage. No one may escape them, no matter how beautiful the vista appears seen through the romantic eyes of love. But couples who have faced these problems in premarital counseling need not be afraid; nor need they cover the future with unrealistic childish hopes. They stand on firm ground. The vows can be said with confidence that theirs will be a life-long union in which they will become "one flesh," able to "love, honor and cherish each other, and so live together in faithfulness and patience, in wisdom and true godliness, that their home may be a haven of blessing and of peace." [3]

Summary

It is my conviction that premarital counseling offers every minister a very unique pastoral function for which he should make special preparation. Because of its far-reaching consequences, it may be the most important part of the pastoral care of his people. There will be those who resist premarital counseling and others who may criticize the minister for discussing intimate marriage relationships. But if the minister will consistently and patiently teach young and old its value, he shall find his reward in its acceptance and in the happy marriages he will help build.

[3] *Book of Common Prayer,* p. 303.

APPENDICES

Appendix I

THE PROTESTANT EPISCOPAL CHURCH

CANON 17

OF THE SOLEMNIZATION OF HOLY MATRIMONY[1]

Sec. 1. Every Minister of this Church shall conform to the laws of the State governing the creation of the civil status of marriage, and also to the laws of this Church governing the solemnization of Holy Matrimony.

Sec. 2. No Minister of this Church shall solemnize any marriage unless the following conditions are complied with:

   (a) He shall have ascertained the right of the parties to contract a marriage according to the laws of the State.
   (b) He shall have ascertained the right of the parties to contract a marriage according to the laws of this Church, and not in violation of the following impediments:
   (1) Consanguinity (whether of the whole or of the half blood) within the following degrees:
      (a) One may not marry one's ascendant or descendant.
      (b) One may not marry one's sister.
      (c) One may not marry the sister or brother of one's ascendant or the descendant of one's brother or sister.

[1] *Constitution and Canons for the Government of the Protestant Episcopal Church in the United States of America,* Canon 17. Of the Solemnization of Holy Matrimony, 1955, pp. 44-47.

(2) Mistake as to the identity of either party.

(3) Mental deficiency of either party sufficient to prevent the exercise of intelligent choice.

(4) Insanity of either party.

(5) Failure of either party to have reached the age of puberty.

(6) Impotence, sexual perversion, or the existence of venereal disease in either party undisclosed to the other.

(7) Facts which would make the proposed marriage bigamous.

(8) Concurrent contract inconsistent with the contract constituting canonical marriage.

(9) Attendant conditions: error as to the identity of either party, fraud, coercion, or duress, or such defects of personality as to make competent or free consent impossible.

(c) He shall have ascertained that at least one of the parties has received Holy Baptism.

(d) He shall have instructed the parties as to the nature of Holy Matrimony.

(e) The intention of the parties to contract a marriage shall have been signified to the Minister at least three days before the service of solemnization; *Provided,* that, for weighty cause, the Minister may dispense with this requirement, if one of the parties is a member of his congregation, or can furnish satisfactory evidence of his responsibility. In case the three days' notice is waived, the Minister shall report his action in writing to the Ecclesiastical Authority immediately.

(f) There shall be present at least two witnesses to the solemnization of the marriage.

(g) The Minister shall record in the proper register the date and place of the marriage, the names of the parties and their parents, the age of the parties, their residence, and their Church status, and the witnesses and the Minister shall sign the record.

Sec. 3. The Minister shall have required that the parties sign the following declaration:

We, A.B. and C.D., desiring to receive the blessing of Holy Matrimony in the Church, do solemnly declare that we hold marriage to be a lifelong union of husband and wife and as it is set forth in the Form of Solemnization of Holy Matrimony in the Book of Common Prayer. We believe it is for the purpose of mutual fellowship, encouragement, and understanding, for the procreation (if it may be) of children, and their physical and spiritual nurture, for the safeguarding and benefit of society. And we do engage ourselves, so far as in us lies, to make our utmost effort to establish this relationship and to seek God's help thereto.

Sec. 4. It shall be within the discretion of any Minister of this Church to decline to solemnize any marriage.

Sec. 5. No Minister of this Church shall solemnize any marriage except in accordance with these Canons.

Sec. 6. No Minister of this Church shall solemnize the marriage of any person who has been the husband or wife of any other person then living whose marriage has been annulled or dissolved by the civil court, except as hereinafter in these Canons provided; or shall any member of this Church enter upon a marriage when either of the contracting parties has been the husband or wife of any other person then living whose marriage has been annulled or dissolved by a civil court, except as hereinafter in these Canons provided.

Mixed marriages

The General Convention of the Protestant Episcopal Church in the U.S.A., 1949, adopted the following resolution presented by the author:

Resolved, that this Convention earnestly warns members of our Church against contracting marriages with Roman Catholics under the conditions imposed by modern Roman Canon Law, especially as these conditions involve a promise to have their children brought up in a religious system which they cannot themselves accept; and, further, because the religious education and spiritual training of their children by word and example is a paramount duty of parents and should never be neglected nor left entirely to others, we assert that in no circumstances should a member of this Church give any understanding, as a condition of marriage, that the children should be brought up in the practice of another Communion.[2]

THE LAMBETH CONFERENCE 1958
THE FAMILY IN CONTEMPORARY SOCIETY
Marriage[3]

The Conference records its profound conviction that the idea of the human family is rooted in the Godhead and that consequently all problems of sex relations, the procreation of children, and the organization of family life must be related, consciously and directly, to the creative, redemptive, and sanctifying power of God.

The Conference affirms that marriage is a vocation to holiness, through which men and women may share in the love and creative purpose of God. The sins of self-indulgence and sensuality, born of selfishness and a refusal to accept marriage as a divine vocation, destroy its true nature and depth, and the right fullness and balance of the relationship between men and women. Christians need always to remember that sexual love is not an end in itself nor a means to self-gratification, and that self-discipline and restraint are essential conditions of the responsible freedom of marriage and family planning.

The Conference welcomes, with thankfulness, the increasing care given by the clergy to preparation for marriage both in instructing youth, through confirmation classes and other means, and also immediately before marriage. It urges that the importance of this ministry should continue to be emphasized and that special attention should be given to our Lord's principle of life-long union as the basis of all true marriage.

The Conference believes that the responsibility for deciding upon the number and frequency of children has been laid by God upon the consciences of parents everywhere: that this planning, in such ways as are mutually acceptable to husband and wife in Christian conscience, is a right and important factor in Christian family life and should be the result of positive choice before God. Such

[2] Journal of the General Convention of the Protestant Episcopal Church in the United States of America, 1949.

[3] The Lambeth Conference 1958 (Greenwich, Conn.: The Seabury Press, 1959), pp. 1.56-1.58, 1.59.

responsible parenthood, built on obedience to all the duties of marriage, requires a wise stewardship of the resources and abilities of the family as well as a thoughtful consideration of the varying population needs and problems of society and the claims of future generations.

The Conference calls upon all Church people to have in mind that, since our Lord's ministry gave a new depth and significance to forgiveness, his Church and the families within it must be a forgiving society, and that there are no wrongs done by its members, one to another, that are unforgivable, or in which a costly forgiveness may not lead to repentance and, through repentance, to reconciliation and a new beginning in living together.

The Conference believes that many tensions in marriage and family life are allowed to reach a breaking point because self-righteousness or a sense of injury takes priority of forgiveness, and that marital relations also break down because those involved do not in time take counsel with a wise advisor. It affirms that no husband or wife has the right to contemplate even legal separation until every opportunity of reconciliation and forgiveness has been exhausted.

The Conference welcomes the growth of Marriage Guidance Councils, which prepare people for marriage and assist in maintaining stable married life. It recommends that the clergy and Church people of mature faith and with the right qualifications should be encouraged to offer themselves for training as consellors. It believes that such counsel, given as a Christian vocation by well-trained Christian husbands and wives, is a volunteer service of great value, makes an important contribution to the community, and deserves government support.

The Conference recognizes that divorce is granted by the secular authority in many lands on grounds which the Church cannot acknowledge, and recognizes also that in certain cases, where a decree of divorce has been sought and may even have been granted, there may in fact have been no marital bond in the eyes of the Church. It therefore commends for further consideration by the Churches and Provinces of the Anglican Communion a procedure for defining marital status, such as already exists in some of its Provinces.

The Conference believes that the Resolutions of the 1948 Lambeth Conference concerning marriage discipline have been of great value as witnessing to Christ's teaching about the life-long nature of marriage, and urges that these Resolutions, and their implications, should continue to be studied in every Province.   [See Chap. 5.]

The Christian family

The Conference commends, as an aid to better teaching about marriage and home life, the following summary of the marks of a Christian family. Such a family:

(a) Seeks to live by the teaching and example of Jesus Christ;
(b) Joins in the worship of Almighty God on Sundays in church;
(c) Joins in common prayer and Bible reading, and grace at meals;
(d) Is forgiving one to another, and accepts responsibility for one another;
(e) Shares together in common tasks and recreation;
(f) Uses abilities, time, and possessions responsibly in society;
(g) Is a good neighbour, hospitable to friend and stranger.

The Conference believes that a most important answer to the crushing impact of secularism on family life lies in a return to the discipline of family prayer and in a faithful common Christian life in the household. It urges that the clergy work towards this end by teaching both the privilege and the means of such worship, and of Bible reading, in which fathers should take their due place with mothers and children as members and ministers of a worshipping community.

The Conference, recognizing that there is a world-wide need for decent and suitable housing, records its belief that every married couple should have adequate privacy and shelter, for the better bringing up of the family as well as for the benefit of its own married life; and that national and local government share fully with private enterprise the community's obligation to meet this need.

The Committee on the Family in Contemporary Society in its report to the Lambeth Conference 1958 stated:

1. THEOLOGY OF SEXUALITY AND THE FAMILY

The purposes of marriage

First of all, the family is rooted in the elemental processes of life itself. Human reproduction—human parenthood—is vastly more complicated than the reproduction of plants or the simpler animals. Mankind has rightly come to see depths and possibilities in the process, and in the relationships which it establishes, which are, at best, only faintly suggested (if indeed they exist at all) in the lower orders of life. Still the human family, even in its richest and noblest complexity, is at one with all of nature in its function as the means by which new life is begun.

The commandment in Genesis to "be fruitful and multiply" reflects this biological function. More significantly, it raises it to the level of God's creative purpose. Underlying the insistent drive of all life to reproduce itself is the creative activity of God himself, who ordered nature in this way and established the process and the urgent impulse, and reveals to mankind something of his purpose in so doing. Indeed, the revelation expressed in Genesis implies that in this fruitfulness, to some degree, man shares in God's creative work, that he is admitted to a quasi-partnership with God in the establishment of new life. Therefore the process of human reproduction, from the earliest levels of Biblical revelation, has been seen as invested with a special and responsible dignity.

The Biblical revelation, however, does not limit the function of sexuality and the family to the reproductive purpose. Equally deep-rooted in Genesis is the reflection of a second factor—the need of man and woman for each other, to complement and fulfil each other and to establish a durable partnership against the loneliness and rigour of life. It was not good for man to be alone, and God made a helpmeet for him. This relationship of man and woman—of husband and wife—is rooted in God's creative purpose equally with the procreative function of sexuality. "For this reason shall a man leave his father and mother and be joined to his wife." [4]

[4] Gen. 2.18-25; Matt. 19.4f.

Thus, in the heart of the Biblical teaching about creation, two great insights into the nature and purpose of sexuality and the family are lodged. They are not subordinated one to the other; they are not directly related to one another; their relationship, in the developing experience of Israel, is to be found in yet a third area—that of the place of the family in giving responsible security to the children born of the love of husband and wife. . . .

Christ's teaching about marriage deals directly with only the second of the three purposes mentioned, that of the personal relationships between husband and wife. . . . The tie between husband and wife is, by God's ordinance, a life-long one, not to be broken by any act of man. In his answer he quotes two texts from Genesis: that God created sexuality in mankind ("male and female created he them"), and that the right relationship between the sexes was the union, life-long and life-deep, of the two in "one flesh." [5]

To summarize, three purposes—three functions—are interwoven in human sexuality. Each of them is profoundly rooted in human experience and in God's revelation. The procreation of children, the fulfilment and completion of husband and wife in each other, and the establishment of a stable environment within which the deepest truths about human relationships can be expressed and communicated and children can grow up seeing and learning what mature life is really like—these are the great purposes which, in God's loving will, marriage and the family are created to serve.

Relationship between the purposes

It has been common, in Christian theology, to mention the procreative function first, as if to say that it is the ruling purpose. So it is, in the sense that no marriage would be according to God's will which (where procreation is possible) did not bear fruit in children. But it is clearly not true that all other duties and relationships in marriage must be subordinate to the procreative one. Neither the Bible nor human experience supports such a view. Where it has been held, the reason generally lay in a fear of the misuse of the sexual relationship or in a false sense that there is, in any sexual relationship, an intrinsic evil. Neither fear nor a false sense of

[5] Gen. 1.27; 2.24.

what is "evil" is a helpful guide for humanity, in this or any other matter.

Responsible parenthood is both a more complex relationship and a far richer one than merely the reproduction of the species. Granted that the institution of the family is inescapably rooted in the biology of procreation and that this must always form part of the moral structure within which the decisions of husband and wife must lie, still the heart of family life—the heart of the marriage which is the cornerstone of the family—is the responsible freedom of the partners who make the marriage to begin with.

Indeed the whole enterprise of marriage and the establishment of a family is perhaps the most vivid expression we know of responsible human freedom under God. A man and a woman, free and competent to do so, agree before God and society to take each other as husband and wife, without reservation, for life. Any such adventure of free people carries with it both the privilege and the obligation of making the choices with which life confronts us.

Marriage does not merely happen to us. It is something for which Church and State can only provide the setting and the protections of law and doctrine. It is something which husband and wife create and maintain, with the help of God, by means of the multitude of choices of which the day-to-day texture of a marriage is woven. Indeed it is those very choices which are signified by the promises "to love and to cherish," for love is something people *do* far more than merely something they feel; it is an act of the will as well as—often before—it is an emotional experience. And the most important of all those choices are those which involve the fundamental purposes of marriage and family life.

This is no new discovery. What is new, in our society, is the well-nigh fatal ease with which those purposes can now be separated from one another. It was suggested earlier that in God's revelation there is no automatic unity among them. This is paralleled in human experience everywhere, which has taught us how easy it is to dissociate sexual pleasure from the sober duty of procreation, and to sever them both from the third group of obligations of family loyalty. To keep all three sets of relationships and duties together, in one frame of moral reference, is an art man has had a long fight to learn, and must still steadily fight to preserve. This

unity or harmony of purpose in marriage can never be taken for
granted: it is always threatened by sin and ignorance—and never
more so than in our time.

Techniques and devices for controlled conception now make it
generally and easily possible to plan for parenthood at will. Thus
the old, direct relationship between sexual intercourse and the
procreation of children has been broken. The fear which has so
often dominated sexual intercourse has largely disappeared, and with
it many of the accustomed disciplines of sexual conduct. And, in
this new situation, there appear new problems for conscientious
choice, and new possibilities for the marital relationship. . . .

The commanding problem, as was said above, is the problem
which every husband and wife faces, of maintaining a right relationship among the three great purposes of their marriage. The two
most critical areas for this are, first, the question of family planning
and, secondly, that of the permanence of the marriage bond.

Family planning

The responsible procreation of children is a primary obligation.
The questions, How many children? At what intervals? are matters on which no general counsel can be given. The choice must
be made by parents together, in prayerful consideration of their resources, the society in which they live, and the problems they face.

It may be said, however, that responsible parenthood implies
a watchful guard against selfishness and covetousness, and an
equally thoughtful awareness of the world into which our children
are to be born. Couples who postpone having children until certain financial goals are reached, or certain possessions gained, need
to be vigilant lest they are putting their own comfort ahead of their
duty. Similarly, those who carelessly and improvidently bring children into the world, trusting in an unknown future or a generous
society to care for them, need to make a rigorous examination of
their lack of concern for their children and for the society of which
they are a part.

In general, the earlier in a marriage children are born, the better
—both for them and their parents. And there is every reason to
suggest to young men and women that is is far wiser to postpone

marriage for a time than to enter it in constant fear of accidental pregnancy. Sexual relationships scarred by fear are tragically incapable of bearing either the strains or the joys of full and happy married life.

But the procreation of children is not the only purpose of marriage. Husbands and wives owe to each other and to the depth and stability of their families the duty to express, in sexual intercourse, the love which they bear and mean to bear to each other. Sexual intercourse is not by any means the only language of earthly love, but it is, in its full and right use, the most intimate and the most revealing; it has the depth of communication signified by the Biblical word so often used for it, "knowledge"; it is giving and receiving the unity of two free spirits which is in itself good (within the marriage bond) and mediates good to those who share it. Therefore it is utterly wrong to urge that, unless children are specifically desired, sexual intercourse is of the nature of sin. It is also wrong to say that such intercourse ought not to be engaged in except with the willing intention to procreate children.

It must be emphasized once again that family planning ought to be the result of thoughtful and prayerful Christian decision. Where it is, Christian husbands and wives need feel no hesitation in offering their decision humbly to God and following it with a clear conscience. The *means* of family planning are in large measure matters of clinical and aesthetic choice, subject to the requirement that they be admissible to the Christian conscience. Scientific studies can rightly help, and do, in assessing the effects and the usefulness of any particular means; and Christians have every right to use the gifts of science for proper ends. . . .

In the man-woman relationship, not only before marriage but in it, chastity and continence are virtues of positive worth, sustained by the grace of God, for they release creative power into other channels. If the sexual relationship is to be truly an expression of partnership, the male has to recognize that his sexual urge may be the stronger and therefore he has more consciously to exercise self-control. Nothing that is said hereafter about the use of contraceptives in family planning takes away from the beauty and strength of abstinence mutually accepted.

Some of the means which are not acceptable to Christians are listed, together with the reasons for that judgement, as guides to parents in their choices:

The wilful withholding of one partner from intercourse with the other, sometimes mis-named "continence," cannot be endorsed, for such persistent one-sided denial of the right of bodily love of husband and wife is a denial of one of the supreme conditions and purposes of marriage as God has established it. . . .

The Christian conscience rightly rejects any means which interrupts or prevents the fulfilment of coitus and thus precludes, in husband or wife, the full completion of the sexual act.

In the strongest terms, Christians reject the practice of induced abortion, or infanticide, which involves the killing of a life already conceived (as well as a violation of the personality of the mother), save at the dictate of strict and undeniable medical necessity. . . .

The Christian rightly accepts the help of responsible physicians in making conception possible, where it may be prevented by some physical or emotional abnormality. Artificial insemination by anyone other than the husband raises problems of such gravity that the Committee cannot see any possibility of its acceptance by Christian people. . . .

The question of sterilization, whether therapeutic, genetic, or contraceptive in its intent, presents a complex ethical problem. . . .

The Committee agreed that sterilization when an imperative medical necessity (as in hysterectomy or the treatment of cancer) is justified. . . .

Voluntary sterilization, either as a government policy or only as an individual choice, raises many grave questions. . . .

The choice of sterilization is a grave one, to be made only in deepest and most conscientious thought, with full agreement between the spouses. . . .

The discussion of these specific questions has illustrated the complexity of the choices husbands and wives are daily called upon to make. They have a duty to bear children; they owe an equal duty to each other, of tender and completing love; and these two duties interpenetrate and lighten each other. Neither one should master the other, for then marriage is distorted and untrue. To keep them both in true balance is never easy, and the use of effective contraceptives, with its persistent invitation to sensuality and selfishness, is an added hazard.

Yet to say this is to say no more than that no human relationship or dignity is easy to achieve. Marriage is a vocation as well as an estate of nature; it is an essay in responsible freedom; and we have no more right to expect it to be without its problems than we might expect good citizenship or personal integrity to be painless. Freedom is the condition of every human virtue and of every grace.

Freedom is also the way towards the attainment of all that is excellent and true. And, perplexing though the choices in contemporary marriage are, it must also be said that the new freedom of sexuality in marriage in our time is also, and equally, a gate to a new depth and joy in personal relationships between husband and wife. At a time when so much in our culture tends to depersonalize life—to erode and dissolve the old, clear, outlines of human personality—Christians may well give thanks for the chance given us to establish, in marriage, a new level of intimate, loving interdependence between husband and wife and parents and children, freed from some of the old disciplines of fears.

It must be said once more that this will not happen automatically. It will happen only when we deliberately choose it, and pay the cost of it in self-discipline, in courtesy towards one another within the marital tie, and in willingness to receive and give the fullest communication of love, physically as well as in every other way. . . .

Christian family ideals

* * *

In a true family, children learn that there is one God. They learn it first from their parents, and from the disciplined and thoughtful obedience parents and children alike pay to the same God. Parents who force on a child an obedience they are not willing to accept equally for themselves are committing one of the deepest offences of family life, for they are giving to their child a false view of the one God who rules over all life and in whose will is our peace.

In a true family, children learn what love and judgement mean, for a family ideally is a society in which all bear common pain and share common grief, and all give and receive equally of love.

In a true family, children learn, little by little, how to be free; they practise how to make the choices life requires of them, within the protection of loving concern and watchful care.

In a true family, children learn the essential standards of judgement—how to tell the important things, how to distinguish the true and the excellent and the right, how to speak rightly and listen with courteous love.

In a true family, children learn how to accept themselves and, in time, how to accept others on the same basis; for membership in a family comes not by earning it nor buying it, nor is it given only to those who deserve it. Like life itself and the grace of God, it comes without deserving; and the self-acceptance of healthy childhood is a precious preparation for a humane and tolerant manhood.

In a true family, children learn how to be themselves, in true individuality, and how to accept others in their equally true individuality, with patience and kindness.

Of such qualities is a true family made. To bear witness to these things is part of the vocation of a Christian family in our society. In that society, sympathetic to its good influences, critical of, or resistant to, its unwholesome influences, the truly Christian home should be salt and leaven. To be this it has to be sure of itself and of its basis in the will of God and the Gospel.

Such a home is the one place where Christians can live by the Gospel, as they cannot fully do in a society where other sanctions come in. The marks of "living by the Gospel" are the care of each for other, the value set on persons for their own sake without regard to merit or demerit, to success or failure. Where there is this warm understanding and love there is both freedom and responsibility. Each member feels free to be himself. This sense of freedom is one of the marks of a Christian in the world—all too rarely found in Church or in society.[6]

[6] *The Lambeth Conference 1958*, pp. 2.142-2.152.

Appendix II

DOCTRINES AND DISCIPLINE
OF THE METHODIST CHURCH 1956

352. The duties of a pastor are:

*   *   *

6. To instruct youth in the problems involved in marriage with a member of a church which demands that the children of such marriage be reared in the faith of that church.[1]

*   *   *

355. In planning to perform the rite of matrimony the minister is advised to have an unhurried premarital conference with the parties to be married. It is strongly urged that the minister have this conference at least several days before the date of the wedding, and that the minister advise and instruct to the best of his ability to the end that the parties to be married become soberly aware that successful marriage is dependent on those spiritual qualities which are best nurtured and kept alive by a constant sense of loyalty to God and to God's organized Church.[2]

[1] *Doctrines and Discipline of the Methodist Church 1956,* (Nashville, Tenn.: The Board of Publication of the Methodist Church, Incorporated, © 1957), p. 127.

[2] *Ibid.,* p. 130.

356. No minister shall solemnize the marriage of a divorced person whose wife or husband is living and unmarried; but this rule shall not apply (1) to the innocent person when it is clearly established by competent testimony that the true cause for divorce was adultery or other vicious conditions which through mental or physical cruelty or physical peril invalidated the marriage vow, nor (2) to the divorced persons seeking to be reunited in marriage. The violation of this rule concerning divorce shall be considered an act of maladministration.[3]

THE FOLLOWING RESOLUTION WAS ADOPTED BY THE GENERAL CONFERENCE OF 1956

2021. The Christian Family

The modern family is struggling against great difficulties: the tensions created by the world situation, uncertainties due to the present military demands on youth, inadequate housing, uprooting of families due to unprecedented population shifts, and the coarsening influence of many mass media on the lives of children. The end result of these difficulties is evidenced by the high rate of divorce, juvenile delinquency, broken lives, and a general laxity of moral standards. It is only when the family fulfills its highest functions and is truly Christian that its members rise above these difficulties and thus aid in halting the trends threatening the home.

The home is the place where emotional weaknesses of the members of the family come to light, where children express their innate hunger to be secure, to belong, to be needed, to be recognized.

Religion and the family naturally belong together. What religion is to accomplish it can do best in the family. What the family must do, it cannot do without religion. Religion and the family are natural allies. Religion is inseparable from the family. Family life at its best is a matter of living life at the deepest level, which is a level of relationship to God.

1. *What Is a Christian Family?* A Christian family is one in which parents so live the Christian life and practice the presence of God that children come to accept God as the greatest reality of life.

[3] *Ibid.*, p. 130.

A Christian family is one in which each member is accepted and respected as a person having sacred worth.

A Christian family is one that seeks to bring every member into the Christian way of living.

A Christian family is one that accepts the responsibility of worship and instruction to the end of developing the spiritual life of each person.

A Christian family is one that manifests a faith in God, observes daily prayer and grace at meals, is committed to behavior in keeping with Christian ideals for family relations, community life, and national and world citizenship.

2. *Religion and the Family.* The undergirding love of God, as taught by Christian parents, by word and example, is one of the greatest sources of emotional and spiritual security for the growing life. Where the awareness of God is present, families will find opportunities for informal experience of prayer in many situations of life. The beauties of nature, the joys of comradeship, the tragedies of bereavement, the elation that comes with good fortune, the facing of common problems—all these can be shared with God in the simple words of prayer.

In addition to these moments of informal religious expression, the Christian family will provide for planned periods of worship. This will include the participation in leadership by children as well as by adults. There is no substitute for the Bible as a central aid to worship when parents read it with appreciation for the growing needs of children. We recommend the use of such resources for worship as *The Christian Home, The Upper Room,* and the devotional materials in the church-school literature.

3. *Marriage Relations.* Marriage is an achievement. It doesn't just happen. It comprises a growing oneness in which emotional adjustments from time to time are affected by an understanding of right ways of living together.

a) Preparation. It is increasingly obvious that if marriage is to succeed, there must be adequate preparation. Therefore, it is recommended that a regular course of instruction for youth on the Christian ideals of friendship, courtship, and marriage be given in each local church, using the available materials. In our youth assemblies, camps, and institutes qualified persons should give counsel on personal problems, social relations, and the duties and privileges of Christian marriage. Suitable books, pamphlets, and audio-visual resources should be made available for young people. It is further recommended that courses of instruction for young married couples on home building, income budgeting, child training, life adjustments, and personality problems be given by each local church.

The time has come when every person planning marriage should have the opportunity for skilled and careful counseling by ministers or staff workers who are prepared in this field. If this is to be done, pastors must be trained to guide young people through premarital and postmarital counseling.

b) Mixed Marriages. Religious conviction should be a strong tie in marriage. Recent research has emphasized the importance of common cultural and religious background as the foundations of successful marriage. It is therefore strongly urged that each young person consider carefully before becoming engaged to anyone who does not have a similar religious background. It is important that Protestant youth discuss this problem with their ministers before it is too late. Ministers are urged to discuss with both youth and parents the likelihood of failure in mixed marriages.

c) Planned Parenthood. We believe that planned parenthood, practiced in Christian conscience, may fulfill rather than violate the will of God.

d) Divorce. Divorce is not the answer to the problems that cause it. It is symptomatic of deeper difficulties. The church must stand ready to point out these basic problems to couples contemplating divorce, and help them to discover and, if possible, to overcome such difficulties. In addition, the church must stand ready to depict the unhappy circumstances that are to await the divorced person. As a Christian church, and as ministers, we are obligated to aid, by counsel, persons who have experienced broken marriage, and to guide them so that they may make satisfactory adjustments.

4. Relationships in the Home. It is living together within the family that is the final test of religious living. The highest qualities are found in the life and character of Jesus Christ; these must be manifest in daily family living.

If we want to help the children in our homes develop, there must be an inner acceptance of each child. He must be loved for himself with all the limitations he may possess. In each instance he must be treated as an individual.

a) Parent-Child Relations. We recognize that parents are constantly teaching in the home in unrecognized ways as well as in their conscious efforts. Parents, in co-operation with the churchschool teachers, should make possible the Christian education of their children throughout the week. There is great need for parents to interpret to their children in a Christian way the present world issues and needs, the politics of national and international relationships, the efforts of the people of the world through the United Nations to do those things which make for peace and more abundant life, the complex problems created by the use of beverage alcohol and narcotics, and the need for adhering to Christian moral standards amid the tensions and pressures of our present-day living. There is also need for parents to guide their children in learning how to evaluate the propaganda to which they are constantly subjected through newspapers, magazines, radio, television and movies. At these points the church and the family can support and strengthen each other in their ideals of personal conduct and social righteousness.

b) Co-operation. We recommend that our churches co-operate with other agencies in the community that are working for the improvement of family life and for the strengthening of Christian character. The National Conference on Family Life has demonstrated one way in which the boards and agencies of the church can work together for the promotion of Christian family living.

c) Sex Education. Parents must assume the responsibility of interpreting to each child, before his adolescence, the facts regarding the origin of life. If properly instructed, parents are best fitted to educate their children in regard to sex; but if they have been negligent, then qualified persons in the church should reverently teach the beautiful truths of life. We recognize that sex education is not mere information. It includes also the formation of attitudes and habits.

d) Mass Media. Parents must also help their children evaluate literature and radio and television programs which come into the home and counteract the undesirable publicity brought into the home through these mass media in terms of Christian and wholesome attitudes, to the end that their children will develop a taste for the best.

e) Three-Generation Families. In the family there must be a recognition of the older adult. Medical science is making life increasingly longer. Older adults need and should have a significant place of recognition as members of the family circle.

5. *The Church and the Family.* The church and the family need each other. Through their support of the church, parents teach by example the importance of the church in the life of the nation. When they neglect the church, they teach their children that the church is of little importance in the lives of people.

To help parents understand the importance of teaching in the home, and the best methods for guiding their children, it is recommended that local churches make provision for study classes and discussion groups on child development, family relationships, and the teaching of religion in the home, using the helpful materials provided through the regular publications of the church.

There is value in all the members of the family worshiping together both in the home and in the church. It is expected that local churches will provide resources and help for the family worship experiences. Churches are encouraged to hold occasional special services at which the entire family can worship together, with the service planned for the participation of all age groups.

It is important for the churches to focus attention on the family at frequent intervals during the year. Especially do we recommend the observance of National Family Week as provided in 250 & 5.

Parents and teachers are urged to meet together frequently to discuss the Christian nurture of children and ways in which they can work together for better teaching. Parents are urged to read together with their children the lesson materials provided by the church. Teachers are urged to keep parents informed regarding the objectives of the lesson materials and to point out ways in which parents can further these objectives through home participation.

6. *Legislation.* To protect both the individual and society from hasty marriages we favor legislation requiring a period of days or weeks between the application for a marriage license and the

granting of it. This will allow sufficient time for consideration on the part of the two persons concerned. We also favor a longer interval between application for and granting of divorce.

We recommend laws requiring a medical examination of both contracting parties, and the refusal of a license to those unfitted physically or mentally by heredity or otherwise for the responsible state of matrimony.

We further favor uniform marriage and divorce laws.[4]

[4] *Ibid.*, pp. 707-712.

Appendix III

AMENDMENT TO THE CONFESSION OF FAITH OF THE PRESBYTERIAN CHURCH IN THE UNITED STATES ENACTED BY THE GENERAL ASSEMBLY 1959

CHAPTER XXVI*

OF MARRIAGE AND DIVORCE

1. Marriage is a union between one man and one woman designed of God to last so long as they both shall live.[1]

(1) Gen. 2:23,24; I Cor. 7:2,39; 13:8,13; Matt. 5:31,32; 19:4-6 (Mark 10:5-9); Eph. 5:28,31,33; Romans 7:2,3.

2. Marriage is designed for the mutual help of husband and wife,[2] for the safeguarding, undergirding, and development of their moral and spiritual character;[3] for the propagation of children and the rearing of them in the discipline and instruction of the Lord.[4]

3. All persons who are able with judgment to give their consent may marry,[5] except within the limits of blood relationship forbidden by Scripture,[6] and such marriages are valid before God in the eyes of the Church.[7] But no marriage can be fully and securely Christian in spirit or in purpose unless both partners are committed to a

---

* *Minutes of the Ninety-Ninth General Assembly of the Presbyterian Church in the United States,* Atlanta, Georgia, April 23-28, 1959, pp. 69, 70.

common Christian faith and to a deeply shared intention of building a Christian home. Evangelical Christians should seek as partners in marriage only persons who hold in common a sound basis of evangelical faith.[8]

(2) Gen. 2:18,24.

(3) Gen. 1:27,28; 2:18-25; I Cor. 7:3-5,9,36; Eph. 5:22-23; Col. 3:18,19.

(4) Gen. 1:27,28; 9:1; Mal. 2:15; Matt. 18:5,6,10,14; 19:14 (Mark 10:13-16, Luke 18:15-17); Eph. 6:1-4; Col. 3:20,21.

(5) Gen. 1:27,28.

(6) Lev. 18:6-18; Mark 6:18; I Cor. 5:1.

(7) Mark 1:30; John 2:1,2; I Cor. 7:7,36; 9:5; I Tim. 4:3; 5:14; Heb. 13:4.

(8) I Cor. 7, especially v 39; II Cor. 6:14,15.

4. Marriage for the Christian has religious as well as civil significance.[9] The distinctive contribution of the Church in performing the marriage ceremony is to affirm the divine institution of marriage;[10] to invoke God's blessing upon those who enter into the marital relationship in accordance with His Word;[11] to hear the vows of those who desire to be married; and to assure the married partners of God's grace within their new relationship.[12]

(9) Prov. 18:22; Matt. 19:6; Mark 10:9,11,12; Eph. 5:29,30,32.

(10) Gen. 1:27,28.

(11) Mark 10:9.

(12) Eph. 5:22,23.

5. It is the Divine Intention that persons entering the marriage covenant become inseparably united, thus allowing for no dissolution save that caused by the death of either husband or wife.[13] However, the weaknesses of one or both partners may lead to gross and persistent denial of the marriage vows so that marriage dies at the heart and the union becomes intolerable; yet only in cases of extreme, unrepented-of, and irremediable unfaithfulness (physical or spiritual) should separation or divorce be considered. Such separation or divorce is accepted as permissible only because of the failure of one, or both, of the partners and does not lessen in any way the Divine Intention for indissoluble union.[14]

6. The remarriage of divorced persons may be sanctioned by the Church in keeping with the redemptive Gospel of Christ, when sufficient penitence for sin and failure is evident, and a firm purpose of and endeavor after Christian marriage is manifested.[15]

7. Divorced persons should give prayerful thought to discover if God's vocation for them is to remain unmarried, since one failure in this realm raises serious question as to the rightness and wisdom of undertaking another union.[16]

(13) Gen. 2:23,24; Matt. 5:31,32; 19:4-9; Mark 10:5-9; Romans 7:2,3; I Cor. 7:2,10,11,39; 13:4-13; Eph. 5:28,31,33.

(14) Matt. 19:7-9; Mark 10:4-9; I Cor. 7:12,13,15.

(15) II Sam. 12:13; Neh. 9:17; Ps. 32:5; 130:4; Matt. 12:13a; 21:31,32; Luke 7:36-50; 15:11-32; John 3:16,17; 8:3,11; Romans 3:23; 10:9,10; Gal. 6:1; I Tim. 2:4; Heb. 7:25; I John 1:9, 2:1,2.

(16) Matt. 5:31,32; Mark 10:11; Luke 16:18; I Cor. 7:10,11,20,32-35.

THE BOOK OF CHURCH ORDER
OF THE PRESBYTERIAN CHURCH IN THE UNITED STATES 1945*

371. Marriage is a divine institution, though not a Sacrament, nor peculiar to the Church of Christ. It is proper that every commonwealth, for the good of society, make laws to regulate marriage, which all citizens are bound to obey.

372. Christians should marry in the Lord; therefore it is fit that their marriage be solemnized by a lawful Minister, that special instruction be given them, and suitable prayers offered, when they enter into this relation.

373. Marriage is to be between one man and one woman, in accordance with the Word of God.

374. The parties should be of such years of discretion as to be capable of making their own choice; and if they be under age, or live with their parents, the consent of the parents or others, under

* *The Book of Church Order of the Presbyterian Church in the United States* (Richmond: John Knox Press, 1945), pp. 193-194. Used by permission.

whose care they are, should be previously obtained, and well certified to the Minister before he proceeds to solemnize the marriage.

375. Parents should neither compel their children to marry contrary to their inclinations, nor deny their consent without just and important reasons.

376. Marriage is of a public nature. The welfare of civil society, the happiness of families, and the credit of religion are deeply interested in it. Therefore, the purpose of marriage should be sufficiently published a proper time previous to the solemnization of it. It is enjoined on all Ministers to be careful that, in this matter, they transgress neither the laws of God, nor the laws of the community; and that they may not destroy the peace and comfort of families, Ministers should be assured that, with respect to the parties applying to them, no just objections lie against their marriage.

THE FOLLOWING STATEMENT WAS ADDED TO PARAGRAPH 376
AT THE NINETY-NINTH GENERAL ASSEMBLY 1959 *

1. It shall be the responsibility of the minister who is asked to officiate at a marriage to provide adequate time for careful premarital counseling with the parties involved. Attention shall be given to all important aspects of marriage, especially those where problems may arise, whether they be physical, emotional, economic, social, moral or religious. In some instances the minister may deem it wise to refer the couple to a physician or other qualified person for special counseling. The minister shall carefully instruct the couple in the Standards of our Church as set forth in chapter XXVI of *The Confession of Faith* and in this chapter of *The Directory for Worship*. This counseling procedure shall be followed not only for those contemplating marriage for the first time, but also for any who may be seeking remarriage. In every instance it shall be the minister's duty to assist the couple in laying firm foundations for the establishment of a Christian home.

2. A true and lasting marriage can be achieved only when its physical bonds are reinforced and sanctified by a variety of moral

* *Ibid.*, pp. 70-71.

and spiritual ties: respect, affection, common ideas and interests, the unselfish wish of each partner for the other's welfare in all things, and a mutual sharing of the common joys, griefs, opportunities and burdens of the home. This means that both faithfulness and un-faithfulness in marriage must be conceived in spiritual as well as physical terms.

But, while both physical and spiritual fidelity are vital, and while both are essential to the attainment of marriage at its best, husbands and wives should bear in mind that human weakness and frailty may manifest themselves in this realm as in all others. They should, therefore, cultivate the Christian graces of understanding, patience, generosity, repentance and forgiveness. They should re-member that just as other human relationships can survive imper-fections, so can marriage. Our Lord's command to forgive and, if need be, to forgive repeatedly, is especially applicable in this inti-mate and delicate relationship. The offending partner should not look upon forgiveness of the other as license to keep on sinning but should regard this forgiveness as a summons to repentance and as the ground of reestablishing harmony within the union.

3. When marriage seems in danger of breaking for any cause, per-manent separation or divorce must always be regarded as a last resort. Neither can rightly be sanctioned by the Church except where a continuation of the legal union would endanger the physi-cal, moral or spiritual well being of one or both of the partners or that of their children. Thus, every Christian minister will view as a vital pastoral responsibility the duty of preventing, so far as he can, by wise and prayerful counsel, the hasty or ill-considered separation or divorce of any couple committed to his care.

4. When a Christian who has been divorced applies to a minister for remarriage, the minister's chief concern shall be the applicant's present fitness of heart and life for the intended marriage. The supreme test of this fitness should be one's honest purpose to profit from past experiences and to plan and work for a Christian home on soundly spiritual foundations. Careful attention should also be given to the applicant's psychological readiness for a new mar-riage experience. If the applicant has been clearly and grossly wronged by a previous mate, this fact may incline the Church to allow and sanction the remarriage without further question, but the

mere fact of having been wronged will not necessarily mean that the applicant understands fully the spiritual demands of marriage and holds to a high and serious purpose to make the coming marriage Christian. The minister, therefore, shall take care to be as fully satisfied on the latter point as on the first. On the other hand, if the applicant has been clearly at fault in the break-up of the earlier marriage, or is found even to be chiefly at fault, the mere fact of previous guilt (however grievous) should not be held as a rigid and final disqualification for remarriage under the auspices and with the sanction of the Church. Here, too, the minister shall weigh, as of paramount importance, the quality of the applicant's present faith, contrition and purpose, being mindful always of the infinite mercy of God and careful never to hold against any honest child of God a sin which God Himself may have forgiven and put behind Him forever. In a word, in all cases where remarriage is sought, the minister's decision shall turn not so much on what the applicant has done but rather on what this person by God's grace has now become, and what, with God's help, he (or she) honestly intends and hopes to do in the future.

5. The Session of each church may appoint a committee to advise with the minister in all cases where divorced persons make application for remarriage. The minister may seek the advice of this committee and after a careful investigation on the basis of our Church's Standards and a conscientious consideration of all pertinent facts may approve or decline the request. Normally, the applicants should appear before the committee to state their case and declare their intention to establish a Christian home.

6. The Presbytery may appoint a committee on remarriage to which may be referred cases upon which the minister or the Session feels it may be better qualified to render a decision.

7. In all instances of the remarriage of divorced persons the officiating minister shall, before solemnizing the marriage, seek definite assurance that the attitude of the parties toward their new marriage is in accordance with the fundamental doctrines of our Church.

377. The Minister should keep a proper register of the names of all persons whom he marries, and of the time of their marriage, for the perusal of all whom it may concern.

Appendix IV

The United Lutheran Church in America adopted the following statement on Marriage and Family Life at the 1956 Convention:*

1. Marriage is that order of creation given by God in love which binds one man and one woman in a lifelong union of the most intimate fellowship of body and life. This one-flesh relation, when properly based on fidelity and love, serves as a witness to God's grace and leads husband and wife into service one of the other. In their marriage husband and wife are responsible to God for keeping their vows and must depend upon his love and mercy to fulfill them.

2. God has established the sexual relation for the purpose of bringing husband and wife into full unity so that they may enrich and be a blessing to each other. Such oneness, depending upon lifelong fidelity between the marriage partners and loving service one of the other, is the essential characteristic of marriage. Marriage should be consummated only in love with the intention of maintaining a permanent and responsible relation. Continence outside of marriage and fidelity within marriage are binding on all.

---

* *Minutes of the Twentieth Biennial Convention, 1956,* The United Lutheran Church in America (Philadelphia: The United Lutheran Publication House, 1956), pp. 1145-1146.

3. Procreation is a gift inherent in the sex relation. In childern the one-flesh idea finds embodiment. Children bring great joy to marriage and reveal how God permits men to share in his continuing creation. Married couples should seek to fulfill their responsibilities in marriage by conceiving and nurturing their children in the light of Christian faith.

4. Husband and wife are called to exercise the power of procreation responsibly before God. This implies planning their parenthood in accordance with their ability to provide for their children and carefully nurture them in fullness of Christian faith and life. The health and welfare of the mother-wife should be a major concern in such decisions. Irresponsible conception of children up to the limit of biological capacity and selfish limitation of the number of children are equally detrimental. Choice as to means of conception control should be made upon professional medical advice.

5. Marriage, as ordained by God, is a lifelong indissoluble union consummated through consent and coitus. Any breaking of the marriage bond involves sin and suffering. Forgiveness and reconciliation are incumbent upon all within marriage, and especially upon Christians. The church should extend its counseling services in an effort to maintain and strengthen families when they face difficulties threatening their unity.

6. Where marriage failure and divorce occur among Christian people, the church should recognize its involvement in the failure and seek to lead all concerned in repentance and forgiveness. If it proves impossible or unwise in the light of Christian love and concern for the welfare of all involved to reconstitute the marriage, then the church should continue, insofar as possible, to minister to each person involved.

If the question of the remarriage of a divorced person arises, pastors and congregations of The United Lutheran Church in America should make their decisions on the particular circumstances in each case, being guided by the following considerations:

(a) While it is the Christian teaching that marriage is a lifelong, indissoluble union and that divorce and remarriage do violate God's order, nevertheless, God in his love does accept the sinner and deals with him according to his need. The church has recognized that marriage may be a remedy for sin and has seen in such Bible passages as Matthew 5:32; 19:9 and I Corinthians 7:15 the possibility of remarriage, but it also knows that the final basis of decision is loving concern for man in his actual situation.

(b) The divorced person seeking remarriage must recognize his responsibility in the breakup of the former marriage. He must give evidence of repentance and have made an effort to overcome his limitations and failures. He must have forgiven his partner in the former marriage, and he and his intended spouse must give assurance that he will fulfill his obligations to those involved in his former marriage.

(c) The divorced person must give evidence of his Christian faith by his witness in the church and must have received adequate counsel and training in preparation for marriage. He must be prepared to undertake the full responsibilities of marriage in dependence upon God.

7. The church should provide opportunities for its pastors and lay leaders to prepare themselves to meet their responsibilities in ministering to families, and to young people contemplating marriage. This involves seminary training, in-service training opportunities, college courses, and special courses and institutes for lay leaders. Study material based on the view of marriage set forth in these summary statements should be provided.

8. Congregations should provide opportunities for study courses and other activities in preparation for marriage. Help should be given through activities strengthening and enriching the life of existing family groups. Each pastor should require regular counseling periods with couples before marriage. In part this may be done with groups, but private and individual conferences should also be required.

9. Congregations and youth auxiliary and student groups of the church should continue to carry on educational programs regarding the special problems in mixed marriages. The inevitable compromise or denial of the evangelical faith, and the social and

cultural problems usually accompanying such marriages, should be thoroughly explained.

10. The wedding service is a service of the church in which the atmosphere of reverence and worship should be maintained. The recognized service of the church should be used, and only such activities as are in conformity with the Christian view of marriage and in keeping with a service of worship should be permitted.

* * *

12. In order to develop the highest standards of pastoral practice regarding marriage and family life synods should hold conferences of pastors for discussion and clarification of the pastoral practices envisaged in this study.

13. Christian citizens should seek the enactment of uniform and constructive marriage and divorce laws. Such laws should encourage the procedures of adjustment and reconciliation rather than adversary litigation.

Appendix V

HOLY MATRIMONY

Date of Application _____ 19__

Groom's Full Name _____

Residence _____

Occupation _____

Bachelor or Widower _____ Color or Race _____

Number of this Marriage _____

Baptized _____ In what denomination _____

Communicant _____ In what denomination _____

Age ____ Date of Birth _____
                        Month   Day   Year

Place of Birth—City _____ State _____

Father's Name _____

Mother's Maiden Name _____

* May be ordered from Morehouse-Barlow Co., 14 E. 41st Street, New York 17, N.Y. Reproduced by permission.

Parents' Residence _____

Bride's Full Name _____

Residence _____

Occupation _____

Maiden or Widow _____ Color or Race _____

Number of this Marriage _____

If Widow, Give Maiden Name _____

Baptized _____ In what denomination _____

Confirmed _____ In what denomination _____

Communicant _____ In what denomination _____

Age _____ Date of Birth _____
                           Month   Day   Year

Place of Birth—City _____ State _____

Father's Name _____

Mother's Maiden Name _____

Parents' Residence _____

License No. _____ Where Issued _____

Date of Ceremony _____ Hour _____

Place of Ceremony: Church _____ Chapel _____ Residence _____

Holy Communion _____ Organist _____ Choir _____

Rehearsal _____ Flowers _____ Fees _____

Names of Witnesses—1. _____

                    2. _____

Permanent Address After Marriage _____

Officiant _____

Appendix VI

Marriage Council OF PHILADELPHIA, INC.

3828 LOCUST STREET • PHILADELPHIA 4 • PENNSYLVANIA

Serial No. _____

Partner's Code _____   **BACKGROUND SCHEDULE**

NAME _____ DATE SCHEDULE IS FILLED IN _____

PRESENT ADDRESS _____

PERMANENT ADDRESS _____

Place where you are while filling in this schedule (Marriage Council office, class, elsewhere) _____

Please be sure to answer every question. In answering them, DRAW A CIRCLE AROUND THE NUMBER IN FRONT OF THE APPROPRIATE RESPONSE, or put a check mark where called for. Do not circle more than one alternative unless asked to do so.

1 SEX
1—Male
2—Female

2 RACE
1—White
2—Negro
3—Other

3 Give your age at time of filling this schedule:
_____ years _____ months.

4 What was your birthplace?
1—Born inside U. S. A. (specify state) _____
2—Born outside U. S. A. (specify country) _____
3—Do not know

5 Birthplace of your parents
FATHER
1—Born inside U. S. A.
2—Born outside U. S. A. (specify country) _____
3—Do not know

MOTHER
1—Born inside U. S. A.
2—Born outside U. S. A. (specify country) _____
3—Do not know

6 What is your marital status at time of filling in this schedule? (Be sure to circle only one alternative).
1—Single, not engaged
2—Single, engaged, or going steady
3—Married
4—Widowed
5—Separated (because of friction) or divorced
6—Other (for example, common law marriage)

7 If married,
(a) What was the date of your marriage?

_____ _____ _____
Month   Day   Year

(b) How many children do you have? _____
(c) Children's birthdates and sex

_____ _____
_____ _____
_____ _____

IN ANSWERING QUESTIONS 8, 9, 10, 11 and 12, YOU WILL BE ASKED ABOUT YOURSELF AND YOUR PARTNER (IF YOU ARE ENGAGED OR MARRIED). IF YOU DO NOT HAVE A PARTNER, IGNORE PARTNER'S COLUMN.

8 In what religion were you and your partner brought up?
Yourself Partner
1 _____ 1 _____ Protestant
2 _____ 2 _____ Roman Catholic
3 _____ 3 _____ Jewish
4 _____ 4 _____ Other (specify) _____
5 _____ 5 _____ No organized religion
6 _____ 6 _____ Do not know

9 What is your religion and what is your partner's religion at the time of filling in this schedule?
Yourself Partner
1 _____ 1 _____ Protestant but not active
2 _____ 2 _____ Protestant and active
3 _____ 3 _____ Protestant and very active
4 _____ 4 _____ Catholic but do not attend
5 _____ 5 _____ Catholic and attend occasionally
6 _____ 6 _____ Catholic and devout
7 _____ 7 _____ Jewish but do not attend
8 _____ 8 _____ Jewish and attend High Holidays
9 _____ 9 _____ Jewish and attend regularly
0 _____ 0 _____ Other, not active (specify) _____
1 _____ 1 _____ Other, active (specify) _____
2 _____ 2 _____ Other, very active (specify) _____
3 _____ 3 _____ No organized religion
4 _____ 4 _____ Do not know

10a Have you or your partner been, or are either of you now in military service?
Yourself Partner
1 _____ 1 _____ Yes
2 _____ 2 _____ No

10b If either of you have been in military service give date of entering.

Yourself..
　　　　Month　　　　　Day　　　　　Year

Partner..
　　　　Month　　　　　Day　　　　　Year

Date of Discharge

Yourself..
　　　　Month　　　　　Day　　　　　Year

Partner..
　　　　Month　　　　　Day　　　　　Year

11 Circle the alternative which best describes the number of years of school or college which you have completed and which your partner has completed at the time of filling in this schedule. (Do not include any vocational training such as nursing, secretarial training, etc. in answering this question.)

Yourself　Partner

1　　　1　　　8 years of school or less

2　　　2　　　9 or 10 years (1 or 2 years of high school)

3　　　3　　　11 or 12 years (3 or 4 years of high school)

4　　　4　　　13 or 14 years (1 or 2 years of college)

5　　　5　　　15 or 16 years (3 or 4 years of college)

6　　　6　　　17 and over (post graduate or professional education)

7　　　7　　　Do not know

12 Circle any of the following types of vocational training which you may have had in addition to the above.

Yourself　Partner

1　　　1　　　None

2　　　2　　　Nursing

3　　　3　　　Secretarial

4　　　4　　　Other (specify) _____

13 Are you now a student?

1—Yes—Give name of institution_____

2—No

14 What was the longest period in years you lived in one residence before you were 21?_____years

15 Did you share in the housework when you were growing up?

1—No

2—Yes, occasionally

3—Yes, frequently

16 Do you like domestic activities now?

1—Like very much

2—Like somewhat

3—Slight dislike

4—Considerable dislike

17 In general, in what activities do you participate at the present time? Check one of the three columns for **each** of the following activities.

	Never or Seldom	Sometimes	Often
Motion pictures			
Dances			
Competitive sports (playing tennis, etc.)			
Spectator sports			
Outdoor activities (riding, walking, fishing, etc.)			
Social gatherings with friends (to play cards, talk, etc.)			
Reading			
Art appreciation (listening to music, play-going, visiting art exhibits, etc.)			
Creative and interpretive art (writing, drawing, acting, singing, playing a musical instrument, etc.)			
Politics			
Hobbies (collecting, mechanics, woodwork, needlework, etc.)			
Membership in clubs and organizations (school or college clubs, national organizations, etc.)			
Business or professional activities (beyond office hours)			

18 Occupational classification of your _father_ as you were growing up (or of the person who supported the family)

1—No employment history
2—Unskilled worker
3—Semi-skilled worker (garage attendant, bench hand, farm hand, etc.)
4—Skilled worker (automobile mechanic, toolmaker, draftsman, police, fireman, engineman, etc.)
5—White-collar worker (file clerk, typist, salesman, secretary, bookkeeper, clerk, etc.)
6—Small business man (retailer, garage operator, etc.)
7—Professional worker (teacher, minister, doctor, lawyer, artist, musician, regular army or navy officer, etc.)
8—Business executive or professional administrator
9—Farmer
0—Not applicable (Brought up in institution, etc.)

19 What is _your_ occupational classification at time of filling in this schedule? (Circle the appropriate classification below and specify the exact title of your job here
_____)

1—Not employed for compensation (circle here for housewife, student, retired, etc.)
2—Unskilled worker
3—Semi-skilled worker (garage attendant, bench hand, farm hand, etc.)
4—Skilled worker (automobile mechanic, toolmaker, draftsman, police, fireman, engineman, etc.)
5—White-collar worker (file clerk, typist, salesman, secretary, bookkeeper, clerk, etc.)
6—Small business man (retailer, garage operator, etc.)
7—Professional worker (teacher, minister, doctor, lawyer, artist, musician, regular army or navy officer, etc.)
8—Business executive or professional administrator
9—Farmer

20a In the family in which you were raised, were there children other than yourself? (Include all other children raised in your household)

1—No other children
2—Yes (specify number irrespective of whether they are now living or not_____)

20b List the present ages of living brothers and sisters below:—

Brothers ___ ___ ___ ___ ___
Sisters ___ ___ ___ ___ ___

21 What was your position among your brothers and sisters, according to order of birth? (Include all other children raised in your household)

1—Only child
2—Oldest child
3—Youngest child
4—Intermediate child

22 On the whole, while you were growing up, how happy were you?

Before your teens / During your teens
1—Very happy / 1—Very happy
2—Happy / 2—Happy
3—Unhappy / 3—Unhappy
4—Very unhappy / 4—Very unhappy

23 When you were 16 or 17 years of age, how many boy companions did you have?

1—None or a few
2—Fair number
3—Many

24 When you were 16 or 17 years of age, how many girl companions did you have?

1—None or a few
2—Fair number
3—Many

25 What is the present marital status of your own parents? (Be sure to circle only one alternative)

1—Married
2—Separated (because of marital friction)
3—Divorced, neither remarried
4—Divorced, father remarried
5—Divorced, mother remarried
6—Divorced, both remarried
7—Widowed, not remarried
8—Widowed, remarried
9—Neither living
0—Other

26 If your own mother is living, check here_____
If your own mother is not living, how old were you when she died?_____years

27 If your own father is living, check here_____
If your own father is not living, how old were you when he died?_____years

28 If your own parents are not separated or divorced, check here_____
If your own parents are separated or divorced, how old were you when this occurred?_____years

29 How would you describe your own parents' relationship to each other (or the relationship of the adults with whom you grew up)?

1—Warmly affectionate and demonstrative
2—Affectionate but reserved
3—No signs of affection
4—Not applicable—Comment _____

30 To what extent were your parents in disagreement (or the adults with whom you grew up)?

1—In conflict all the time
2—Alternately fighting and making up
3—Tolerated each other without conflict
4—No conflicts apparent
5—Do not know
6—Not applicable

31 Appraisal of the happiness of your own parents' marriage (or the adults with whom you grew up)

1—Very happy
2—Happy
3—Unhappy
4—Very unhappy
5—Do not know
6—Not applicable

32 How did you get along with your own mother?

Before your teens (approximately up to age 12)	During your teens (approximately ages 12-19)	At present time
1—Very well	1—Very well	1—Very well
2—Fairly well	2—Fairly well	2—Fairly well
3—Poorly	3—Poorly	3—Poorly
4—Cannot say because mother not living or did not have contact with her during this period.	4—Cannot say because mother not living or did not have contact with her during this period.	4—Cannot say because mother not living or do not have contact with her now.

33 How did you get along with your own father?

Before your teens (approximately up to age 12)	During your teens (approximately ages 12-19)	At present time
1—Very well	1—Very well	1—Very well
2—Fairly well	2—Fairly well	2—Fairly well
3—Poorly	3—Poorly	3—Poorly
4—Cannot say because father not living or did not have contact with him during this period.	4—Cannot say because father not living or did not have contact with him during this period.	4—Cannot say because father not living or do not have contact with him now.

34 Did you get along with one parent better than the other?

Before your teens (approximately up to age 12)	During your teens (approximately ages 12-19)	At present time
1—Got along better with mother or her substitute	1—Got along better with mother or her substitute	1—Get along better with mother or her substitute
2—Got along better with father or his substitute	2—Got along better with father or his substitute	2—Got along better with father or his substitute
3—Got along with both parents equally well	3—Got along with both parents equally well	3—Get along with both parents equally well
4—Not applicable	4—Not applicable	4—Not applicable

35 Was your home with your own parents broken by death, divorce or separation?

1—Yes
2—No

IF YOU ANSWERED NO TO THE ABOVE QUESTION (35), THE REMAINING QUESTIONS DO NOT APPLY TO YOU. THEREFORE, YOU DO NOT NEED TO ANSWER THEM UNLESS YOUR RESPONSE WAS YES.

36 If your home was broken (you answered yes to question 35) with whom did you live afterward?

1—Lived with father
2—Lived with mother
3—Lived with relatives other than father or mother
4—Lived in home other than relatives
5—Lived in institution
6—Lived alone (boarding house, etc.)
7—Other (specify) _____

37 If one of your parents remarried before you were 21, and you lived with that parent during that period, give your appraisal of the happiness of the remarriage.

1—Not applicable
2—Very happy
3—Happy
4—Unhappy
5—Very unhappy
6—Do not know

38 If you have lived with a step-mother, foster or adoptive mother, how did you get along with her?

Before your teens (approximately up to age 12)	During your teens (approximately ages 12-19)	At present time
1—Not applicable	1—Not applicable	1—Not applicable
2—Very well	2—Very well	2—Very well
3—Fairly well	3—Fairly well	3—Fairly well
4—Poorly	4—Poorly	4—Poorly

39 If you have lived with a step-father, foster or adoptive father, how did you get along with him?

Before your teens (approximately up to age 12)	During your teens (approximately ages 12-19)	At present time
1—Not applicable	1—Not applicable	1—Not applicable
2—Very well	2—Very well	2—Very well
3—Fairly well	3—Fairly well	3—Fairly well
4—Poorly	4—Poorly	4—Poorly

Appendix VII

In the Name of the Father, and of the Son,
and of the Holy Ghost. Amen.

DECLARATION OF INTENTION [1]

We,

_____
and

_____

desiring to receive the blessing of Holy Matrimony in the Church,
do solemnly declare that we hold marriage to be a lifelong union
of husband and wife as it is set forth in the Form of Solemnization
of Holy Matrimony in the Book of Common Prayer.

We believe it is for the purpose of mutual fellowship, encouragement, and understanding, for the procreation (if it may be) of
children, and their physical and spiritual nurture, for the safeguarding and benefit of society.

And we do engage ourselves, so far as in us lies, to make our
utmost effort to establish this relationship and to seek God's help
thereunto.

_____
signature of groom

_____
maiden name signature of bride

Dated _____ A.D. _____

[1] See Appendix 1.

BIBLIOGRAPHY

Bibliography

Books

Amstutz, H. Clair, *Growing Up to Love.* Scottdale, Pa.: Herald Press, 1956.

Baber, Ray E., *Marriage and the Family*, 2nd Ed. New York: McGraw-Hill Book Co., Inc., 1953.

Bergler, Edmund, *Conflict in Marriage.* New York: Harper & Brothers, 1949.

———, *Unhappy Marriage and Divorce.* New York: International Universities Press, 1946.

Bertocci, P. A., *The Human Venture in Love, Sex, and Marriage.* New York: Association Press, 1949.

Bibby, H. C., *How Life Is Handed On.* New York: Emerson Books, Inc., 1947.

Bowman, Henry A., *Marriage for Moderns*, 3rd Ed. New York: McGraw-Hill Book Co., Inc., 1954.

———, *A Christian Interpretation of Marriage.* Philadelphia: The Westminster Press, 1959.

Burgess, Ernest W. and Paul Wallin, *Engagement and Marriage.* Chicago: J. B. Lippincott Co., 1953.

Butterfield, Oliver M., *Planning for Marriage.* Princeton, N.J.: D. Van Nostrand Co., Inc., 1956.

225

Butterfield, Oliver M., *Sex Life in Marriage*. New York: Emerson Books, 1937.

Cady, B. C. and V. M. Cady, *The Way Life Begins*. New York: American Social Hygiene Association, 1948.

Cole, William Graham, *Sex and Love in the Bible*. New York: Association Press, 1959.

De Schweinitz, Karl, *Growing Up*. New York: The Macmillan Company, 1953.

Dickerson, R. E., *Growing into Manhood*. New York: Association Press, 1954.

Duvall, E. M., *Facts of Life and Love for Teen-Agers*. Rev. Ed. New York: Association Press, 1956.

——, *In-Laws: Pro and Con*. New York: Association Press, 1954.

—— and Reuben Hill. *When You Marry*. Boston: D. C. Heath and Co., Inc., 1953.

Erickson, Clifford E., *The Counseling Interview*. Englewood Cliffs, N.J.: Prentice-Hall, Inc., 1950.

Exner, M. J., *Sexual Side of Marriage*. New York: W. W. Norton, 1932.

Fishbein, Morris and Ernest W. Burgess, *Successful Marriage*, Rev. Ed. New York: Doubleday and Company, 1955.

Franzblau, Abraham, M. D., *The Road to Sexual Maturity*. New York: Simon and Schuster, Inc., 1954.

Greenblat, Bernard R., *A Doctor's Marital Guide for Patients*. Chicago: The Budlong Press, 1957.

Gruenberg, S. M., *The Wonderful Story of How You Were Born*. New York: Hanover House, 1952.

Hiltner, Seward, *Pastoral Counseling*. New York: Abingdon-Cokesbury Press, 1949.

Kirkpatrick, Clifford, *The Family*. New York: The Ronald Press Company, 1955.

Lambeth Conference 1958. Greenwich, Conn: S.P.C.K. and Seabury Press, 1958.

Landis, Judson T. and Mary G. Landis, *Building a Successful Marriage*, 3rd Ed. Englewood Cliffs, N.J.; Prentice-Hall, Inc., 1958.

Landis, Judson T. and Mary G. Landis, *Personal Adjustment: Marriage and Family Living*, 2nd Ed. Englewood Cliffs, N.J.: Prentice-Hall, Inc., 1955.

———, *Readings in Marriage and the Family.* Englewood Cliffs, N.J.: Prentice-Hall, Inc., 1952.

———, *Youth and Marriage: A Student Manual*, 2nd Ed. Englewood Cliffs, N.J.: Prentice-Hall, Inc., 1957.

Levine, Milton and Jean H. Seligmann, *The Wonder of Life.* New York: Simon and Schuster, Inc., 1952.

Levine, Milton, *A Baby Is Born: the Story of How Life Begins.* New York: Simon and Schuster, 1949.

Mace, David R., *Marriage, the Art of Lasting Love.* New York: Doubleday and Company, 1952.

———, *Success in Marriage.* New York: Abingdon Press, 1958.

———, *Whom God Hath Joined.* Philadelphia: The Westminister Press, 1953.

Mudd, Emily H., *The Practice of Marriage Counseling.* New York: The Association Press, 1951.

———, and Aron Krich, eds., *Man and Wife.* New York: W. W. Norton Company, Inc., 1957.

Olsen, Arthur R., Emily H. Mudd and Hugo Bourdeau, *Readings on Marriage and Family Relations.* Harrisburg, Pa.: The Stackpole Company, 1953.

Pike, James, *If You Marry Outside Your Faith.* New York: Harper & Brothers, 1954.

Popenoe, Paul, *Marriage Is What You Make It.* New York: The Macmillan Co., 1950.

Preston, George H., *The Substance of Mental Health.* New York: Rinehart & Company, Inc., 1946.

Rogers, Carl R., *Client-Centered Therapy.* Boston: Houghton Mifflin Company, 1951.

Shostrom, E. L. and L. M. Brammer, *The Dynamics of the Counseling Process.* New York: McGraw-Hill Book Co., Inc., 1952.

Schultz, G. D., *It's Time You Knew.* Philadelphia: J. B. Lippincott Company, 1955.

Skidmore, Rex A., Hulda Van Steeter Garrett, and C. Jay Skidmore, *Marriage Consulting.* New York: Harper & Brothers, 1956.

Stokes, Walter R., *Modern Pattern for Marriage.* New York: Rinehart & Company, Inc., 1948.

Stone, Abraham and Lena Levine, *The Premarital Consultation.* New York: Grune & Stratton, Inc., 1956.

————, and Hannah Stone, *A Marriage Manual.* Rev. Ed. New York: Simon and Schuster, 1952.

Truxall, Andrew G. and Frances E. Merrill, *Marriage and the Family in American Culture.* Englewood Cliffs, N.J.: Prentice-Hall, Inc., 1953.

Van Keuren, Floyd, *Christian Marriage.* New York: Morehouse-Barlow, 1949.

Wood, Leland, F. and R. L. Dickinson, *Harmony in Marriage,* 2nd ed. New York: Round Table Press, 1949.

Pamphlets

Kirkendall, L. A., *Understanding Sex.* Chicago: Science Research Associates, 1947.

Lerrigo, Marion O. and Helen Southard. The following pamphlets were published by the American Medical Association in 1955: *Finding Yourself, Learning About Love, A Story About You, Parents' Privilege, Facts Aren't Enough.*

Sources from which pamphlets may be obtained:

American Institute of Family Relations, 5287 Sunset Blvd., Los Angeles 27, Calif.

American Social Hygiene Association, 1790 Broadway, New York 19, N. Y.

Child Study Association of America, 132 East 74th St., New York 21, N. Y.

Children's Bureau, United States Department of Health, Education, and Welfare, Washington 25, D.C.

Commission on Marriage and the Home, National Council of

Churches of Christ in America, 297 Fourth Ave., New York 10, N. Y.

Family Service Association of America, 192 Lexington Ave., New York 16, N. Y.

National Association for Mental Health, 1790 Broadway, New York 19, N. Y.

National Council on Family Relations, 1219 University Ave., S.E., Minneapolis 14, Minn.

Planned Parenthood Federation of America, Inc., 501 Madison Ave., New York 22, N. Y.

Public Affairs Committee, 22 East 38th St., New York 16, N. Y.

Science Research Associates, 57 West Grand Ave., Chicago 10, Ill.

Superintendent of Documents, United States Government Printing Office, Washington 25, D.C.

INDEX

Index

233

20764

About the Author

J. KENNETH MORRIS is well qualified to write this manual. He was educated at the University of Alabama, Columbia University, the Episcopal Theological Seminary in Virginia, and received a graduate degree in psychology from the University of South Carolina. He is a member of the American Psychological Association, the American Association of Marriage Counselors, Inc., and for the last fifteen years has been rector of St. John's Episcopal Church, Columbia, South Carolina.

PRENTICE-HALL, Inc.
Englewood Cliffs, New Jersey
860 • Printed in U.S. of America